Bringing Up Ziggy

Bringing Up Ziggy

ANDREA CAMPBELL

RENAISSANCE BOOKS

Los Angeles

This is not the definitive book on primate behavior. The author neither advocates nor discourages primate ownership, and the experiences depicted in this volume do not constitute advice on monkey care, handling, or training. All monkeys have individual characteristics, and they should be considered as valuable and irreplaceable resources to be handled by experienced professionals or others with a network of support services. All animals should be thought of as potentially dangerous, and the author and publisher assume no liability for the reader.

Library of Congress Cataloging-in-Publication Data
Campbell, Andrea.
    Bringing up Ziggy / Andrea Campbell.
       p. cm.
    ISBN 1-58063-085-5 (hardcover : alk. paper)
     1. Capuchin monkeys as pets—Arkansas—Hot Springs Anecdotes.
    2. Capuchin monkeys—Arkansas—Hot Springs Anecdotes. 3. Campbell, Andrea. 4. Helping Hands (Organization) I. Title.
SF459.M6C36   1999
636.9'85—dc21   99-36199
                                           CIP

10 9 8 7 6 5 4 3 2 1

Design by Susan Shankin
All photos in this book are from the author's private collection.

Published by Renaissance Books
Distributed by St. Martin's Press
Manufactured in the United States of America
First Edition

contents

acknowledgments

I would like to thank all the members on staff at Helping Hands. In addition to the women in my dedication, I also got the chance to meet Laura Clement and Yue Zhen Liu, and I know Helping Hands appreciates their services. A tip of my hat to the other student-helpers and volunteers, the ones I haven't met but I am sure that God knows who they are.

Special kudos to the foster families, without whom there would be no program quite like this. In particular I'd like to acknowledge Sandy and Bert Calhoun, Patti and Marc Brown, Paula and Jeff Puckett, Betty and Vernon Kent, Janice Smallwood, Leslie and Chuck Vogelwede, and the others who have touched our lives.

In addition, I'd like to thank Elaine Warrington for her good patience and advice. My first reader, and our English teacher extra-ordinaire, Elaine taught my children first, then helped me.

A special thank you to Ann Rademacher, a friend and prima-tologist. A more dedicated caregiver would be hard to find.

Thank you, Michael, my husband; Courtney and Jordan, my sons; and Anna, my mother, for being such a good family and making my life—and Ziggy's—the best it could be. You've followed your wife, mother, and daughter through some crazy ideas but it all works out for the better. I love you.

I'd also like to mention the good people at Renaissance Books and thank them for their support and encouragement, but a special debt of gratitude goes to my editor, Brenda Scott Royce, who believes in primates and fought for us within and without.

introduction

"I write to discover what I think."

—DANIEL BOORSTIN

"Some kid," I say aloud to myself and laugh. Bending down, I press my face up against the cold blue bars and ask for a kiss. The monkey baby inside complies by slipping her tongue out and bussing my lips. I love this imp. Never have I had such affection from the procession of dogs and cats whose short lives enriched my childhood. This monkey girl we named Ziggy will live about thirty to forty years, and that fact makes me content. Longevity is fitting in a creature so loving.

I hear a crick-crack-crick as she pushes the lever on what looks like a remote control dressed in primary colors. It's a baby toy, safe for infant mouths and tiny hands. There are more sophisticated toys in the seven-foot-tall cage: a Fisher-Price busy box, a baby tyke's spinner, an empty plastic 2-liter Coke bottle with a clothes pin inside for clatter. Toys for a baby with a *higher level of learning.*

This young primate, not unlike her human brothers, will be raised to adult age, and then will go off into the world to be trained for her life's tasks. She does not really belong to me, and there is the ache. Ziggy is part of an organization that is much bigger than the both of us; she is a Helping Hands monkey. She will become the working arms and legs of a quadriplegic, someone who lives in a wheelchair and cannot move his own limbs. Monkeys like Ziggy live with foster families until they are a good age to be trained by Helping Hands to be aides and companions to wheelchair-bound people.

Quadriplegics are often the victims of a spinal-related injury, like Christopher Reeve, the actor who played Superman. He was thrown from a horse. Now he is trapped in an uncooperative body and must depend on others for most everything: being fed, getting washed and dressed, having his teeth brushed, and coping with day after day spent in a wheelchair.

Like Reeve, the people who receive Helping Hands monkeys face new challenges in accomplishing the everyday activities most people take for granted. Monkeys help not only with daily tasks but also with filling many long hours with meaning. If you could spend the day with Rett and his monkey Spencer, you would see two devoted companions. When Rett is in his wheelchair, Spencer, his monkey helper, rides on his shoulders. When he is in bed, Spencer curls up on Rett's pillow next to his head, wanting to be close to his "Dad." That's why monkeys are such good helpers. When they bond with the quadriplegic, they will spend hours loving their owners and doing simple tasks for them.

Raising a monkey is hard work. I volunteered for this. I chose to become attached to this unique monkey-child. Life before Ziggy was not as interesting. I was not as committed.

In entering into this unique arrangement, I knew I had a lot to learn: *What do capuchins eat? Where would she sleep? What about diapers?* But what I didn't realize then was that the lessons I'd learn along the way went far beyond the ins-and-outs of daily life with a monkey. This is not a story of monkey mischief and furry faux pas, though we have had our share of those. During our extraordinary adventure together, Ziggy has taught me unexpected lessons about love, commitment, and, ultimately, sacrifice. Observing her growth and behavior, along with studying other primate species, has enhanced my understanding of both animal and human nature. The loftiest ideas still spring from man's genius, but we can all learn a thing or two from the monkeys.

This book is a collection of observations and events in our lives, interlaced with accounts of other primates I have met or read about. Rather than recount our tale in a chronological by-the-numbers format, I have fashioned it more like a scrapbook, with cherished memories juxtaposed against the musings they inspired and flights of fancy offsetting some more serious episodes. The other members of the family have also recorded their impressions for posterity, making this a real family effort.

This is our story. Ziggy was born at Discovery Island in Walt Disney World and came to us at five weeks old. I am the only mother she knows.

gotta love me

It's a dirty trick to introduce everyday
observation into an argument.

UNKNOWN

This "monkey see, monkey do" business is vastly overrated. Ziggy is ten years old now and possesses many capabilities, but imitating me or what I demonstrate to her is not her only priority. She just wants things.

Right now I'm amused by her wanting to participate in the little middling chores of personal human maintenance. If I have a Q-tip, she needs a Q-tip. If I brush my teeth, she wants a toothbrush—to eat paste. This year she started to file her own nails and she makes gimme noises when I pull out the emery board and she has no tools of her own. So I started giving up a nail file every time I do mine, and I watch.

She seems happy working, scraping away against the rough
board, sanding down nails on both fingers and toes. Of course she
knows what to do with it; she's watched me a hundred times. She
runs her nails against it and licks off the powdery dust. File, lick, file,
lick. Think manicures are only for people? Then, when the sand is
gone from the paper, she breaks it in half and the job is done.

Even being the sentimentalist I am, I don't believe I taught her
that. She would have done it without the demonstration. In any event,
let's not for a moment consider her for a job as manicurist. Her threshold of boredom is too short for good service. Plus, creating hangnails
by picking at my cuticles bit by bit is one of her favorite pastimes.

Good grooming aside, along the way I learned there are some
other, more important lessons that primates can teach each other.

Cebus monkeys—Ziggy's Latin name is *Cebus apella*—have large
brains for their body size. Their tool use, foraging strategies, and
what could only be called *deception,* suggest that they are more intelligent than most other animals. There is no other way to put it:
Primates are fairly brilliant. And this is not a story about your usual
dog or cat scenario unless you know of a cat who uses sign language
or a dog who likes to draw on the sides of its cage with chalk.

I'm going to take the hard, unpopular line between animal and
behavioral study and tell you I have learned lessons about certain
aspects of human life and its illusions from a monkey—a "step-
down" primate who has always been represented on the evolutionary tree as an underling, a lesser of man. Most scientists frown upon
this concept, which is referred to as anthropomorphism—giving
human characteristics such as emotion, consciousness, thought, and
motivation to a nonhuman, *an animal.* But then, we as an order—
a category of organisms—are labeled "human primates," and I have

an embarrassing story to tell you about men of science that renders their judgment questionable, at least in my eyes.

Would you believe that as recently as the 1980s, it was routine to perform surgery on infants without anesthesia, using only paralytic dulling agents? Today we'd call that truancy from good common sense, but then it was believed that babies' immature nervous systems were impervious to pain! This outdated, commonly held belief is just one example of how a systematic medical disregard for what others feel can occur. Such insensitivity is not one of the qualities I would care to ascribe to any primate.

In the Name of Science

Scientists believe that studies of monkeys have contributed significantly to our understanding of attachment and nurturing behavior in humans. Some of these studies, though, have taken on cruel, somewhat tortured parameters. Psychologist Harry Harlow performed a series of experiments in which infant rhesus monkeys were raised with artificial mothers made up like wire figures. Some had soft covers and attachments for feeding bottles; some did not.

A report of Harlow's study states, "Harlow then tested infants in mildly fear-provoking situations analogous to those that evoke attachment responses in human children to see if the presence of the artificial mother alleviated the infant's distress." In other words, he scared the bejeezus out of them to see if they clung to their mothers for comfort or if their attachment was strictly one of survival, because she was the source of feeding.

Harlow's work showed that a baby monkey's need was primarily one of comfort and that closeness to the mother figure soothed the

infant in fear-provoking situations. The report goes on to say,
". . . for ethical reasons some experiments simply cannot be performed on humans." The fact that inherently cruel techniques like
this, intended only to prove a point, are deemed necessary at all baf-
fles the mind. I could have told Harlow what he wanted to know.

Because part of the definition of the word *lesson* reads "something, usually unpleasant, which serves as a warning or example," we
should not ignore the often offensive and wayward incentives of men
and women simply because it shames us to think of these actions as
human. We cannot ignore the basic emotions as demonstrated by all
primates. So while we are mapping out which gene makes us fat and
what kind of DNA strand fans a disease like cancer, we have to consider our motives. When you take up the red pencil and examine the
historical script of life, it's only then that you can realize that we have
the uncut, rough drafts of actual life, and we are still not certain how
primate behavior plays a part in it; and that understanding our
motives is vital to growth, maturity, and change.

BECOMING THE MONKEY LADY

To tell you *why* I have a monkey it would be helpful to explain my
state of mind at the time and the chain of events that led to getting
one. For this we have to trip back to the summer of 1986. I was
thirty-seven years old, wife to a husband the same age, and mother to
two boys, ages six and nine. We had just had a foreign exchange
daughter graduate from high school and she was on her way back to
Holland when a personal tragedy struck me down.

A rare form of tumor was discovered growing in the jawbone
under my left ear and lodged almost to the middle of my chin.

Procedures theretofore unknown to me would alter a life I had come to believe was fairly comfortable and active, turning the next four years into hell. The diseased part was cut out and replaced with my own "ilium" (hip bone), which eventually broke from the stress and, subsequently, after two and a half years of orthodontia, was replaced with pieces from my own skull.

It seemed to me throughout this interminably long time that I was always either recovering from a surgery or waiting for another to take place. As my life volleyed between adrenaline and urgency and grief and boredom, it made a minor career singing in a dinner club no longer possible. So *What,* I asked myself, *would I do?*

It is during times of crisis that most of us take stock and reevaluate our lives. It was no different for me. I felt I needed to somehow try to milk some happiness out of this setback. My choices were binary: recuperate and create work . . . or not. Unfortunately, the area I lived in was not ripe with entrepreneurial opportunities, especially for someone with limited parameters—my mouth was wired shut for up to ten weeks at a time and there were frequent trips to Dallas, every six weeks, for two and a half years—so what would I do?

Eventually, the obligatory doctor's visits dwindled down to none. "Go home," they said, "we're done." And after a six-year stint of placing foreign exchange students petered out, I decided to get a real job, something I could do as an at-home cottage industry, and still remain close to bed and the comfort needed for recuperating. So I began to write.

After tons of rejections, some less than well-paid articles, and the unscripted dues all writers have to pay, I eventually found a niche writing career profiles for educational magazines. I was good at explaining a "day in the life," for interested high school students and their teachers who were concerned with vocational opportunity. I wrote about a hodgepodge of jobs: a chimney sweep, an FBI agent, a crane operator, a federal engraver, on and on, a motley of unusual— but interesting—personalities.

One day while trolling for subject ideas, I came across an article in *Reader's Digest* about a woman who had started a most unlikely venture, that of providing monkeys as helpers for quadriplegics, people who live in wheelchairs and are completely helpless to take care of themselves, hence the prefix "quadri" meaning limited or total disuse of all four limbs.

Through the interview process I learned about Mary Joan Willard, a former student of B. F. Skinner, the famous behavioral psychologist. I soon realized that my interest in this topic extended beyond journalistic curiosity and I found myself applying to be a foster family for a monkey.

The decision met with ecstatic enthusiasm from everyone except my husband, Michael. He was leery of taking on more responsibility after what we'd just been through medically, financially, and emotionally. The stress of my ordeal had clearly taken its toll, and we were more than strained financially and in fear of further jaw surgery. But I convinced him that the monkey would give me something to concentrate on when I was in the doldrums. The rest of the family, my mother included, accepted the idea with unblinking challenge; I guess risk-taking is entwined in the genes.

My personal nature is such that I've always chosen to live on the outer limits of the comfort zone, taking on comparatively strange and mind-expanding tasks by traditional standards. It helps that I had no fear of making egregious mistakes, mostly because I didn't know what kinds of mistakes to make. And I thought that maybe I could help someone who had a life situation worse than mine. I knew I wanted to try . . . to feel *valuable.*

So becoming the "Monkey Lady" in the neighborhood was more than simply an oddity; it was my new focus, a kind of survival tactic. It was a way to make new discoveries about myself and my usefulness, and to create something out of what life had thrown at me.

I didn't make this new decision lightly. I believe in the sanctity of wildlife and, basically, I think monkeys and apes should be left alone where they are found. But I have also seen how fate throws curves and how a quadriplegic's strikes come up fast. In private, I've closed my eyes and imagined being housed in a body that won't cooperate, a body that is totally, utterly dependent on another person for every little task, even down to something as minor as a facial itch. If you've even been caregiver to someone in this state, you understand that a simian companion can not only take care of these practical tasks, but can also provide a certain psychological lift that no human could ever give. It gives me goose bumps to think about it still.

PARENT SKILL

My copy is an old edition published in 1976. The cover is frayed and the pages have been dog-eared to mark important, well-worn passages. Several generations who have grown up on the *Dr. Benjamin Spock Baby and Child Care* book take succor in his comforting reassurance at an awkward time in their own lives. A guide primarily for new parents, the first understanding to be bridged is addressed in an early paragraph called, "How you learn to be a parent."

The fallacy that childcare is an innate function for parents is a notion that is perpetuated all over the world. If it were true, there would be no news reports of mothers who leave their infant children in the car in the grueling heat, resulting in needless tragedy. (I thought everyone knows it is not wise to leave a dog in a car in the summer—even with the window cracked—much less a baby!) Another highly questionable idea is that mothers become nurturing caregivers simply because they possess all the correct emotional and physical attributes required for the job. Furthermore, the assumption that fathers will feel responsibility for offspring because they've fathered them, is, unfortunately, not always the case, as demonstrated by the thousands of "deadbeat dads" who refuse to pay child support for separated children.

Spock tells us that parents don't really learn how to care for children from books and lectures, "though these may have value in answering specific questions and doubts." Referring to literature versus experience, he writes that parents "learned the basics from the way they themselves were handled while they were children." He goes on to explain that our childhood games such as playing house and caring for Barbie and Ken were our ways of practicing what we'd been taught by our own parents and how we'd felt about them. In other words, parenting is best demonstrated.

Getting firsthand information about the parenting job is important: babysit, carry babies, read about babies, borrow a baby, or hang around a new mother. Childcare education should be an indispensable component of our society, not simply because you have to let the commitment of parenting seep into your soul but because babies are high-maintenance people and, once arrived, the process never ends. Ziggy was no different. This was definitely not a pet.

From my own perspective gained from raising Ziggy and studying research done with other primates, I've learned a new set of tricks about mothering that I had not mastered in raising two boys, now young adults, or during the temporary care of two foreign exchange daughters, now young women. Because Monkey Handling 101 is not a course I took in college, and because I'd never had any exposure to a monkey nor to anyone who did, *nor did I even know of anyone who had,* I entered into surrogacy with some trepidation. And for good reason—it's not your usual pet situation.

Even though I'd never been closer to a monkey than the cages poised a mere sixty feet away at the zoo, I'd always had an abiding love of nature and a desire to nurture. So what could go wrong? I learned to trust in myself and in the love that can come from years of working at being a giving parent.

I can still recall my children's excitement at the prospect. One night at a family caucus I asked them, "How would you like to be a foster family?" My oldest, not quite sold on sharing amenities with another exchange student so soon after the last one had left, piped up, "What country are they from?" When I responded that it was for a monkey, there was an enthusiastic response.

At times I still marvel at what an air bubble of an idea it was, and I can honestly say that even now we are *still challenged* by the fact that we've invited a monkey into our family of large pink people. Raising a monkey requires a kind of persistence we had forgotten we needed, now that our own children were older.

When I got Ziggy, she was five weeks old. By coincidence, she was born on our wedding anniversary, May 14. She resembled an infant squirrel in size, except for her head, which was the diameter of a golf ball. She had huge, round jewel-brown eyes with just the smallest bit of ruching between them—like the Worf character on the *Star Trek* series. Below that rested a button-sized nose with small, flared nostrils; a thin, upturned mouth; and, although they're not prominent and some people think they're nonexistent, a set of lips. With looks like that, she could have acted like an insolent baby who's had a steady diet of gleaming faces over the sides of her crib, but in the manner of most capuchin infants, she was quiet and dependent.

We followed her growth and progression by reading the Spock book. The wild and interesting part of using that text as a guide was that Ziggy's maturation process was so swift in comparison to the human examples. While a real-life child would be just beginning to hold up its wobbly head, the monkey baby had already been clinging fast to my wrist for a month and was holding onto other objects. It was like raising a child on fast-forward.

One of the stipulations for raising a monkey baby as part of the Helping Hands program is understanding the commitment and being willing to go through the inevitable hoops as they come up. In order to keep a "hand-reared" infant, the primary foster parent has to spend at least ten to twelve hours a day in close bodily contact until the monkey is *at least* eight months of age. Think of it more as time-intensive childcare and less like keeping a pet.

It's still about bringing a baby into your home. You have to understand the sacrifice and realize that you will give to another the biggest parts of who you are and sometimes doubt the reward. Raising Ziggy reminded me that parenting is largely about putting blood, sweat, and tears into something that is not for yourself. When parents accept responsibility for what their children will eventually become, they are setting a pattern of behavior that will live beyond them, past the grave.

For me, Ziggy will go off to be the love of someone else.

baby on board

The best way to forget about your troubles is
to wear a tight pair of shoes.

ANONYMOUS

I once heard someone say that love, like murder, needs motive, means, and opportunity. So you've probably been thinking to yourself, "How did she get into this nonsense?" or maybe, "This woman is a nut." But before you pass judgment on my sanity, let me explain how this unconventional pairing came to be.

My daily life is patterned like a patchwork quilt. It's a study in contrasts that would make even a tired day care worker empathetic. At times I can sit at my computer and write, a production so good and effortless it feels as if I could spin floss into gold because I am reaping the benefits of a quiet, nurturing environment. At other times, I am assaulted by the rattle of iron bars or pelted on the side of my head with an insouciant pitch of wet food. Sometimes I have to stop to sweep up monkey debris, like a day care worker cleaning up after a troupe of energetic two-year-olds.

I didn't take a course in college where I got to bring home a live but temporary specimen to research a theme paper, and you have to admit that a monkey is not your usual pet. I came into this program in a roundabout backdoor way, which, I'm sure, is the way everybody who becomes a surrogate mother for a monkey enters the program.

SLEEPING IN A DRAWER

To say that we were prepared for Ziggy's arrival would be putting a romantic spin on reality. Our family life would be turned topsy-turvy more times than not from then on.

After the foster family application, and just about the time our hopes of ever getting an infant began to flag, we received notification of a new arrival sometime in the spring/summer of 1989. Monkeys are not as prolific as some other animal species, with a gestation period running about 180 to 200 days, and most females giving birth to only one offspring, although twin births have been known to occur.

The announcement had been pinned to our family bulletin board and had a zillion holes at the top from being read so many times and stuck up again. It read: "Congratulations. You are one of 200 families out of almost 3,000 applications that will be receiving a foster monkey."

As a final step, we were instructed to contact our state wildlife office to find out what the requirements or stipulations for this endeavor might be. We were alerted to the chance of denial for entry in some states. Federal and state agencies frown on private ownership of exotic animals (although Ziggy is not considered an exotic because she was bred in the United States) and for good reason, but an Arkansas wildlife agent assured me they were simply "concerned with the animal's welfare."

Helping Hands had sent us a short manual in preparation of Ziggy's arrival. In those early, pioneering years they must have had a lot of faith, knowing that life is not a Jimmy Stewart movie, yet hoping for the best. The introductory passage contained these words: "Each monkey given to foster parents will behave differently."

They were telling words, more profound than we could have known at the time. That statement, as silly as it may have seemed to us as novices looking for finite answers to the secrets of primate care, really gave us the most basic of clues we would refer to over and over again. It told us we would have to rely heavily on common sense and a sense of stick-to-itiveness because, after all, why shouldn't all animals be as individual as we are? Don't animals have emotional lives; don't they experience love and fear? Aren't they curious about their world? Don't they have a sense of self?

The booklet continued: "Some will wean off the bottle quickly, some will cry and be more difficult to wean. Some will readily wear diapers; some will put up a fight. Some will gain weight rapidly, others more slowly. Some will be active and a real 'handful,' some will be quiet and complacent. There are few absolute rules in being a foster parent. Do not expect this manual to have all the answers."

Caught up in the vapor of baby love, we didn't recognize it then, but I believe the implied message was, *your life will take on a charade atmosphere.*

We had waited eight months for our monkey baby to arrive. A former Arkansas host family, the Calhouns, was making a family trip to Disney World in Florida. Because Ziggy was born in a facility on Discovery Island, it was conveniently arranged for the Calhouns to deliver our baby to us on their way home.

Before their departure, a woman called from the veterinarian's office. They were preparing the monkey baby's health certificate for travel and they asked for her name. My names for animals were always inspired by food products—like Noodles or Crackers; we'd had one puppy named Cocoa. Michael came up with the name Ziggy, I think, after the cartoon character with the pin-dot eyes. As we all sounded it out again and again we knew it would be right. I was still operating with fingers crossed, but I knew that if Mike named the monkey, we were on the way to acceptance of the idea.

The day of her arrival was, in the beginning, memorable for all the wrong reasons. Because I had never seen a monkey up close and there was no way of finding out what the experience would be like, I was frightened and began having second thoughts. It seemed as if I was fighting a personality of my own making that simultaneously wanted to hide behind a comfortable sameness, to have my own face again, and yet was always compelled to enter new and uncharted territory.

I was in this state of limbo when a phone call came from the family delivering our baby. They wanted to set a prearranged meeting place we were not familiar with. Not wanting to upset these people for fear of delay (a paranoid-rejection feeling on my part), I agreed the exchange would take place at the North Little Rock Hilton.

On the big day, Michael and I left the boys at home watching a movie on the VCR and headed to the hotel. During the trip, we had one of our worst fights ever. A combination of factors had led us to a frustrated and extremely frazzled state. The strings attached to an answered prayer. We were driving my late father's unwieldy, full-size van. Typical of a blistering Arkansas summer, the afternoon was hot and muggy, a pea soup kind of day. We were unsure of the location, felt wholly unprepared, and, in our apprehension, became completely lost for quite a long time. We drove up and down unfamiliar streets in less-than-scenic neighborhoods, leery of asking for assistance, yet anxious about making our meeting on time.

Finally, when we were nearly a half hour late for the appointed moment, we unwittingly turned a particular corner and there was the hotel, with the former foster family waiting in the lot for our arrival.

The Calhouns were tired from their trip and the exchange went quickly. The precious little cargo was handed over, along with a tiny baby bottle—the type you feed orphaned birds with—a Minnie Mouse doll, a preemie diaper, and a fond good-bye.

The only real preparation we'd made was parking our Dalmatian over at Grandma's house because the dog fancied herself a supreme hunter and had caught and killed several small animals over the years. We live in the piney woods and her catch was prolific that spring— little squirrels, chipmunks, lizards, and baby rabbits. For safety's sake, K-9 would have to wait until Ziggy was a little bigger before she could return home.

It was hands-off policy for the boys too. I knew the baby needed to bond with me, its foster mother. In retrospect, I realize how diffi- cult it must have been for them to just pat her head and stroke the soft downy hair without being able to pick her up and hold her close. Now, Helping Hands tells its foster family applicants that they exclude families with children under ten years. Young children

deserve to be the primary focus of a family's attention, and the combined demands of a young child and that of a monkey baby could
certainly be overwhelming.

In those early years, my children's contributions were small. For a
while I cut the tops off their old sport socks, pierced two small holes
for legs, and then fashioned another slit along the backside for a tail.
The footwear served as makeshift diaper with the aid of a small safety
pin to hold it together in the conventional manner. This homemade
diaper made Ziggy look like she was wearing Omar the tent-maker's
pants. She wore them until we made a connection with the city hospital. At that time, preemie diapers were not on the retail market.
The purchased variety were definitely more efficient and because all
mammals are subject to dreaded diaper rash and need to be changed
every three hours, just how many socks can one sacrifice to this end?

The next hurdle was finding an area for the baby to sleep. Because
her arrival had caught us more unaware than we would have liked to
admit, we were relieved to discover she was a good baby and slept
through the night quite comfortably in the deepest of my son's bottom chest of drawers. With several inches of bedding, she lay atop
the surrogate-stuffed Minnie Mouse, and we felt this would do until
we could buy a regulation carrier. We *would* do this pronto because
we did not want to chance having an infant capuchin dragging herself out of a drawer and getting underfoot or lost.

Like any new parent, I will admit to many nights spent tucked
into the recliner, dozing, stroking, and sleeping with my little girl
curled up on my chest under my pajamas, her downy fur like a mink
glove against my bare skin.

After the drawer and a temporary layover in a dog kennel, we
borrowed the Calhouns' cage. Its heavy metal rods were welded like a

professional enclosure—a seven-foot-tall cage, big enough for clutter. The lower level has a tray we fill with cedar; the next level is a grate through which debris and droppings fall. We change the tray as you would a birdcage, dumping the cedar chips in the woods when they're soiled. A metal boxlike crate is affixed to the side of the cage, like a kind of sleeping compartment. The bars peak at the top in a dome shape and we painted it a primary blue. Over the years the paint has chipped off to expose a primer gray with patches of electric yellow.

The cage requirements to house an older monkey call for a significant amount of space, located on the living level or in the mainstream of traffic so that the monkey can interrelate, observe, and be a part of a family structure. Our house is a tri-level and Ziggy's "apartment" is situated on the second, greatroom level. Here we fix meals, eat, relax, read from the library walls, watch TV, and generally hang out.

I work here too. My makeshift office is a hutch and the dining room table. Ziggy is parked next to my computer; it's like having a baby in a playpen nearby. We have office space downstairs, but I would not want to be away from her, so, like a gypsy, I work where my love lies. The surrounding area is almost all hard surfaces, a mirrored wall, distressed hardwood floors, and under her cage, one of those large pads you put under a desk to run your chair on.

Just as our house reflects the wear and tear of raising sons, monkey messes over the years have taken their toll. There are flecks of brown dashes overhead from a wet tail—I think of them as paintings on the ceiling. Our hand-rubbed antique walls fit in perfectly with the bite marks on the arms of the yellow leather chair (I didn't realize the boys let this happen when Ziggy was teething). Likewise, the old brown flowered couch has stuffing peaking out of the arms from the years the teens popped in and out; it's often covered with comforters or spreads in our shabby-chic environment. Interior design is wasted on monkeys. Diapers leak, food is tossed around, and monkeys tear and shred most anything organic if you let them. Reality begins in earnest to crowd out imagination.

THE ANDROGYNOUS LOOK

Shortly after Ziggy arrived, we got her health certificate in the mail, which provided her health status, identification number (HH231, an I.D. that is also tattooed on the inside of her thigh), and sex: female. When we had the presence of mind to check, we looked at the genitals of our monkey and could not believe that she was not a "he." In baby capuchins, the male and female sex organs look very similar in shape and size. It isn't until the male monkey gets older and his testicles blossom that definite gender identification is more obvious to an inexperienced observer. We were told, by phone, that if we gently pressed the genital and it split somewhat, we would definitely have a girl. It seems when female monkeys are sent to foster parents many times they have a hard time believing their little girl is not a little guy. Ziggy's physiology and a certain amount of time did indeed bear out her function as a female, and we never made light of another person's questions about sexual identity or mix-ups again.

Biology aside, I think there's another reason that dogs are born as puppies, cats as kittens, and so on. Infants of all varieties are new-life cuddly, warm, baby-smelling, and they possess those trusting eyes that draw us in. But their most endearing characteristic is, I think, the fact that they are helpless. Looking upon something that is new, fragile, and defenseless tugs on an emotional ripcord in all nurturing humans, men included.

A capuchin infant is more helpless at birth than might be expected from its size, relative to that of its mother, and the size of its brain, relative to that of its own body weight. Newborn capuchins are unable to move in directed fashion, to lift their heads, or to track objects visually. Control of the head develops swiftly by two weeks, by which time infants can crawl from their mother's abdomen to her back or vice versa, without assistance. In the wild, mothers usually cuddle their newborns, and an infant may remain on its mother's mid-torso for hours, even in the daytime, if it's still.

Once you understand that these infants exist in the intersection between alertness and sleep such that at six weeks they are asleep probably 30 percent of the time, alert but inactive 35 percent of the time, alert/active 10 percent, and nursing or drowsy the other 25 percent of the time, you know the true time commitment desired for hand-rearing. My infant, weighing in at a mere 484 grams, or just over 16 ounces, developed a sleep pattern that alternated with an alert but inactive state of clinging to my wrist. It is a type of dependency that gets your heart so involved that your brain ignores any signals that warn that this nonhuman primate might be a high-maintenance kind of activity for the next eight to ten months.

Monkeys are born with a terrific gripping capability. Unlike human newborns, who by contrast can only grasp a finger and make trivial movements with their arms and legs, an infant monkey will cling to your wrist for dear life. It's an instinct born of survival. In the wild, infants hang on to their mothers for as long as two years, initially clinging to the abdominal region and later moving onto the back. In many species, mothers continue to nurse infants at a low level until the next infant is born. For these infants, weaning is a long, gradual sacrament often completed only at the birth of the next sibling.

A silent ceremony of affection grew between me and Ziggy—
a human mother and her monkey child. Wearing her like a wrist-
watch for several months reminded me of the classic experiment
wherein junior high school students practice at being mothers or
fathers for the first time. Do you remember? It sounded crazy at
first; the object of affection was either a bag of flour or an egg. The
student-cum-parent had to officially name the egg or flour sack,
dress it, and carry it around as a child, always remembering to set it in
a suitable place to keep it safe from harm.

I spoke with Martha Rice, a long-time home economics teacher
at Fountain Lake High School in Hot Springs, Arkansas, about the
program. Ms. Rice told me the experiment was discontinued at her
school for various reasons, but she'd always felt it was a valuable,
telling experience. "A couple of the students had mishaps, placing an
egg in their pocket for convenience and of course, forgetting it later,
and their baby would break. The boys in the class took it very seriously as it turns out, and we even had an egg patrol, a kind of polic-
ing for parents who had left their egg unattended and were turned
in. They learned a new commitment to responsibility, and there were
even times when they had to hire an 'egg sitter.'"

Like those students, in the beginning I was liable to temporarily
forget that a monkey was attached to my wrist like a furry Timex,
and I performed some complicated tasks, such as spending hours on
the sewing machine. Ziggy would be lulled to sleep by the drone of
the engine, and though she was never in danger, she was blissfully
unaware how close she was to an industrious needle. Later, plagued
by guilt, I'd give my next set of activities with her more time and
attention than usual. Life for us in tandem became a ritual of small,
important moments.

At the end of eight weeks, Ziggy could motor well. She could dismount from my arm and walk on all fours but chose to be sitting, touching, or in close contact with my skin at all times. She often used my arm as a chair. Because I am by nature impatient and by nurture pushy, I did not, at first, deviate from my basic activities. It was not uncommon for me to do all major motor activities—vacuuming, dusting, walking, typing—with Ziggy sound asleep on my wrist.

One of the reasons scientists use monkeys for research is because of their swift maturation process. A man's slow growth, lifestyle changes, and long lifespan make it nearly impossible for any one investigator to study a particular individual through all stages of development—talk about having a lifetime project! Because monkeys and apes mature so fast, and because they are genetically our closest relatives (chimpanzee and human DNA is 98.4 percent identical, so whatever it is that makes us different anatomically must reside in the other 1.6 percent), they are our best bet to learning more about ourselves in one lifetime.

Having raised two children, I can attest that the same stages of growth, such as ability, achievement of "firsts," and certain physiological milestones, are present in this nonhuman primate just as they are with human children; they are simply more convenient to study because they occur faster than pulling a rabbit out of the proverbial hat. One minute it seemed as if Ziggy was beginning to teethe—gums swollen and all manner of objects thrust into the mouth for gnawing—and then voilà, almost overnight, a full set of teeth! An assortment of choppers capable of much damage and rather pointed new incisors appeared. This is when we stocked up on teething rings and toys of the indestructible variety, objects made from heavy plastic with smooth edges and round wheels.

It is also when our relationship with her took on a new perspective.

under
hierarchy's spell

> *. . . There's justice for all but it doesn't*
> *seem to be equally distributed.*
>
> UNKNOWN

After only a few weeks mastering the infant stage we were already entering into new levels of activity. Just when we'd begun to take notice of a new development, it was soon behind a newer, more adventurous endeavor. The young become the young and the restless.

In the beginning Ziggy's finger play was rather crude, but in a proportionately short blink of time our baby was manipulating objects more often and during a larger portion of her day. Soon she was climbing a small plastic basket filled with toys, grabbing and chewing on a Scotch tape dispenser or a tube of diaper ointment, or rearranging cloth and empty film canisters. And sooner or later, everything ended up in her mouth.

Hundreds of studies are done with monkeys every year. In one, they looked at the differences between hand-reared and mother-reared infants and how they moved. One published account tells about a hand-reared infant taking her maiden voyage as a biped at only four weeks! Even though moving from place to place is a shaky proposition for infants, it's clear that the favorable conditions a human mother provides—a familiar setting and a firm, flat, stationary surface to play on—accelerates the monkey's acquisition of confidence and enables more rapid exploration of its environment. In contrast, the field-raised infant's need to cling for support, plus the mother's unpredictable mobility, her posture of continuous carriage, and foraging for food, do not allow the wild primate infant enough stability to follow an early longing to explore on its own.

For Ziggy, we humans began mixing baby cereal with her bottled Similac, and she never hesitated to take on new fuel for a motor that in her active times always seemed to be running on overdrive.

As I came to understand the constant physical contact and the carrying bond that infant monkeys so desperately and instinctually need, I began to wonder, as her primary caregiver, if in the future she would choose to be close to only me. The rest of the family had a desire and a need for nurturing too. I wanted this once-in-a-lifetime experience to be shared by the children as well.

As it turns out, I needn't have worried about the situation while Ziggy was still an infant. Soon the instinctual need to cling to me gave way to a need for affection from the rest of the family, and she chose to have a closeness with everyone else. We even brought our family dog, K-9, who'd been staying with my mother, back into the picture. The dog was never left alone with the monkey because predatory instincts are still there after all, but they learned to interact. In the beginning it was some touching—hands for the monkey, nose for the dog—and a lot of smelling and sizing up. And despite their difference in size, K-9 insisted on trying to smell between Ziggy's legs. Later on the dog would learn a different kind of respect, but for now they were simply mildly tolerant of each other.

Pass the Eyeliner, Please

The things we view with interest in the raccoon are his black glasses and ringed tail; in skunks, it's their stripes we notice first. With Ziggy, it's her cap and pair of black gloves, which give her the appearance of a lady dressed for a formal ball. Her chest is a light caramel color that cascades down to a brilliant red, earning her the nickname of "red string monkey." The ensemble is completed by brown hair lying long and flat on the back, leading to a black tail and black shins, which resemble black knee-top boots. It is her beautiful hands and feet that one can't help but wonder at because they so closely resemble our own—dark brown hands with smooth palms and perfectly formed, brown, human-looking nail tips.

At the other end are feet tremendous in length—a walloping three and a half inches. (Comparatively speaking, it would be like a five-foot-tall human with a size 14 shoe.) Even at a tender age, capuchins' feet are unwieldy like swim fins. Toes as thin and long as fingers and a great toe that curls around objects, gives the term *hanging out* new meaning. Considering that this species is primarily arboreal—living in treetops and inhabiting forests from sea level to altitudes of about 5,000 feet—God outfitted their slender limbs and tails with good purpose.

Because one of the joys of motherhood is bathing the infant, we made a ceremony of it. My youngest, Jordan, was always keen on bath time, getting the supplies and providing a helping hand. We filled a smooth plastic container with mildly tepid water and one squirt of an apple pectin shampoo. I washed her with the tiniest sea sponge. It took mere minutes. Afterward, I bound her up tightly in a towel. Her wet body looked froglike and very fragile. There's something mildly rewarding and mystically nurturing about the power of largeness over a creature so small, and the wetness emphasized that.

Some days we would use a blow dryer and brush her lightly. Her hair was kinky when wet, yet smooth and silky when dry. Ziggy liked the warm jet of air blowing against her body. I didn't realize it then, but later learned that grooming among primates is one of their most important rituals. As Roger Fouts says in his book, *Next of Kin,* which is about his experiences caring for a high-spirited chimpanzee named Washoe, "Grooming is the social glue that holds families and communities together. It provides reassurance, comfort, and bonding."

Monkey mothers will pick through their babies' hair and pull off dirt and insects, real or imagined. But it's not so much about external parasites or even cleaning as it is about socialization: Entire families will take turns petting and combing each other's fur. And according to an internal dominance scale within the troop, monkeys who are more powerful or respected will receive more grooming than the others.

It is no different for us. Ziggy will perch on our shoulders and really go to work, parting the hair, scratching around and looking, pretending to bring things back to her mouth. And we will groom her, too, routing through small hair mats, pulling on her ears—in fact, the ear pulling is her favorite part. A few gentle, well-placed tugs on her ears produce a tongue that peeks out between her lips automatically. It's not a smart-looking expression, but it's meaning is unmistakable: *This feels good.*

PECKING ORDER

By mid-summer Ziggy seemed to be one of us. We had established a routine, careful to keep her schedule of cage cleaning, bathing, feeding, and rocking about the same time every day. She was still clinging to my arm like a fur glove and, being an avid walker, I kept up my routine and developed a case of heat rash on my arm where she snuggled during the walk. The Arkansas summer is an inferno of blistering afternoons, but Ziggy seemed unaffected. I assume that the capuchins' native regions in South America are equally torrid, so she's genetically predisposed to handle the heat.

I didn't pay much attention to it then, but as her life became more stimulating, "Zigster"—as the boys took to calling their "sister"—became more powerful. Her grip was stronger, and she seemed to want to be upside down a lot more, so we accommodated her high-wire proclivity. We would gently hold her by the tail upside-down and she seemed to love it, even balancing a bit off the tops of tables, using her tail as an anchor. A couple of times she'd fall, landing on the floor. We humans would react in alarm, but Ziggy would shake it off and roll into a ball or initiate more rough-and-tumble play. I've since learned that x-rays taken of monkeys and orangutans in the wild show that broken and healed bones are not uncommon.

All monkeys have a language of their own, and we learned Ziggy's intonations and gestures pretty quickly as she taught us her speech through endless repetition. For example, in order to initiate friendly conversation with Ziggy, all one had to do was lip-smack. Typically caps will lower their eyelids some, then tilt their heads back and make a continual, quick, repetitive movement of lips coming together again and again. If you do it correctly, a soft sound ensues that capuchins can hear with great acuity.

We also quickly picked up on her nonverbal cues. One physical sign that told us Ziggy was anxious about meeting someone new was when she scratched. She has a tendency to scratch herself at times of stress or insecurity, similar to the unconscious human reaction of scratching our heads when we're confused. If a friend's initial introduction to her met with nervous scratching, we would tell that person to back off and wait until a later time to "engage." Sometimes we'd suggest that they just hang out, lounging and eating as if they belonged in the house, activities that would get her used to their presence.

People fell like dominoes for her charms. Onlookers would react with a chorus of "Ohs" and "Ahs," or if they were the silent type, a huge grin. Whenever we encountered people who showed an interest in Ziggy, I would indoctrinate them into the world of "monkey talk." There would be several folks huddled round cooing, clicking, and smacking, and the more affectionate of the bunch would stick out their tongues—a sign of genuine affection. It's really the polite thing to do, and if successful will be met with an unbridled demonstration of love.

Sometimes, a teeth-baring approach with a direct stare is antagonistic for monkeys, and Ziggy will back into the corner of her cage and react by screaming. *Very loudly.* I don't know what the decibels are, but it is more irritating than a blender on liquefy and almost impossible to talk around. From my friends at the zoo I've learned that in the great apes' culture, this sort of approach is not recommended and can even be dangerous to the uninformed—something to keep in mind on your next visit to the zoo. Acting quiet, self-contained, and contrite is definitely the best posture.

When Ziggy would react in this manner, we would try to soothe over the unfortunate situation by telling the "intruder" not to take it personally and instructing them to back away. Sometimes this behavior seemed random. Those "spurned" were awfully hurt and it took a great deal of reassuring to pep them up again. On the other hand, if they approached with a soft, high-pitched voice—which Ziggy loves personally—she would chatter right back very quickly and take this as an invitation to show off, sticking her foot or thigh out to be petted, or physically lip-smacking their hands. This was the path we always suggested.

About this time, we noticed a growing trait. A pecking order came into play, what we now know as hierarchy. It was very subtle at first, beginning in her conversation with us and showed up again with certain demonstrative acts. Ziggy was placing us, her own family, in an order of preference. I was still top dog, Michael was number two and gaining, Jordan was number three, Courtney hung-in at four, and K-9 was always on the bottom rung of the totem pole. Unbeknownst to us, this hierarchy situation was a red flag for the future. The kids would competitively taunt each other, "my archy is higher than yours," but soon it would not be a contest. Hierarchy would intensify and play itself out again and again throughout her whole being, and life for those on the bottom was the pits.

PRIMATOLOGY 101

Many people use the terms *monkey* and *ape* interchangeably, unaware of the difference. My husband and I frequent an upscale restaurant called Three Monkeys & a Bronze Gorilla. The first time we dined there, I was excited at the prospect of seeing their art and artifacts. We were seated on the main floor, where overhead hung a tapestry of the "three monkeys," which, in fact, was a depiction of three *chimpanzees* balanced one atop the other. Clearly the proprietors did not know the difference between monkey and ape.

It's pretty simple. There are more than 125 species of monkey and only four species of ape alive today. The most obvious difference is that monkeys have tails, apes do not. Gorillas, chimpanzees, orangutans, and gibbons are all apes. They inhabit only two continents, Africa and Asia. Monkeys outnumber apes and enjoy a much wider range, living on five continents. They reside in South and Central America, southern Europe, northern Africa, the Middle East, and throughout southeast Asia. Knowing this, the name of our favorite restaurant should actually be Three Apes & a Bronze Gorilla.

Monkeys are divided into two main groups, New and Old World. New World monkeys and Old World monkeys represent separate evolutionary histories. I'm probably prejudiced in thinking that the New World types are smarter than the others, and I admit to harboring some nonscientific leanings.

Old World monkeys are the ones you see at the zoo that have bright-colored pads on their buttocks. The pads serve several functions in addition to drawing your sight in like a bull's-eye—think what it does for a male!—but I've always felt these characters were not quite up to the intelligent stuff of the New World types. I may be correct in my assumption because a famous ethologist (animal behaviorist), Frans de Waal, says in his book *Good Natured,* "The capuchin monkey is sometimes referred to as the South American chimpanzee, even though capuchins and chimpanzees are only distant relatives. The two species share traits such as tool use, large brains, and omnivorous diet, slow development, and long lifespan." You can add food sharing to this mix.

The two major divisions are technically called Platyrrhini (New World) and Catarrhini (including Old World monkeys, apes, and humans). French zoologist Etienne Geoffroy de Saint-Hilaire established these names, and the terms refer to the external structure of the nose (*rhini* is from the Greek word for nose). New World monkeys are distinguished from the Old World types by a characteristic flat-nosed appearance. The nostrils in the New World monkeys are wide apart and open to the sides whereas the Old World species have nostrils placed closed together and opening forward.

New Worlds also have long, thin fingers that are especially adaptive for manipulating small objects, and they bear strong flat nails, just like humans. So what about the thumb story? And what is this opposability business that scientists always refer to? Well, different species have a better grasp (pardon the pun) on the situation than others, but basically, the thumbs are not *precisely* opposable but could be ascribed that characteristic because they operate with a pseudo-opposable grip. The difference is that although there is no rotation at the wrist-thumb joint as in actual opposability, through movement with the other extremely long fingers, they meet up with the thumb and one or more fingers for an opposable grasp. I noticed right away that Ziggy sucks her thumb, curling the fingers in a fist. I don't know if this trait is species specific, but she's never outgrown it.

In addition, a monkey's big toe is large and bulbous and can be opposed against the other toes for gripping branches or bars. But too much is made of this "opposable thumb" terminology as if it were the wand to capability; some zoologists argue that it has spurred the evolution of the primate brain. In any event, capuchins have incredible proficiency with their slender fingers, including tool manipulation. I have seen my monkey pick up objects as minuscule as a single kernel of rice, pry the tops off bottles, twist wire, scoop out the pulp of fruits, and despite her smaller-sized fingers, lace her hand within mine in a loving hold.

Capuchin monkeys are sometimes called "ring-tailed monkeys" because they often carry their prehensile tails coiled at the tip. People more commonly know the genus as the "organ grinder monkeys," referring to the time when gypsies and street performers employed capuchins dressed in fez caps and boleros to beg for coins by holding a tin cup while the maestro played a small crank-spun organ.

To further understand this nomenclature and because you will see a few different-looking monkeys, all called capuchins, there are four major species: the *Cebus capucinas;* the *Cebus olivaceus* or weeper capuchin; the *Cebus albifrons;* and the *Cebus apella.* The species are separated by their locale as well as their distinct coloration. If you see a capuchin with a black face and another with a white or orange face and you think they have the same expression, you're right: Both are capuchins, but from different neighborhoods.

Cebus apella are found on the eastern slopes of the Andes and throughout the Amazon basin. They are basically brown in color but the shade differs greatly among individuals. Tufts of hair on the forehead and temples, Ziggy's "punk hairdo," is a characteristic of her species and shows up when they're adults; it's a perfectly chiseled three-cornered buzzcut I would come to comment on and marvel over as Ziggy grew older.

MOTHER'S TIME OFF

As every mother needs to have a little downtime away from her infant, I recall relinquishing a certain amount of care to my husband. I also recollect a particular morning when I caught them in a struggle reminiscent of alligator wrestling as Michael tried to rediaper the "kid" for the first time. I entered the dining room to find a flurry of cotton and shredded diaper fleece practically flying through the air! You would have had to have been there to see my jaw fall open. What had they been doing?

Do not let it be said that infant monkeys do not bear great will, an adequate set of choppers, or a proper set of lungs. In fact, their strength—not strength of will but plain brute strength—is remarkable at any age. In Jane Goodall's book *In the Shadow of Man,* she writes that the average adult male chimpanzee is at least *three times* stronger than a man. I've heard it said that an eight-pound monkey can move a thirty-two-pound concrete block. One capuchin named Andy, an eleven-pound adult male, once moved a box containing sixty pounds of weights. In equivalent terms, I've never heard of a man moving more than five times his weight of anything without wheels.

So here was my husband trying to diaper a fragile-looking monkey who was obviously adding her adrenaline, piss, and vinegar to this particular commotion, and he was making a mess of it. He was completely exasperated with having to string a tail through a small slit while being resisted by two hands, two feet with handlike capabilities, and a prehensile tail acting as a fifth hand, as well as a set of sharp little incisor teeth—ouch!—for good measure. I laughed, Michael shrugged, and Ziggy got rescued. As she climbed into my arms I got a tongue kiss and I think I heard Michael say, "You kiss with that mouth?" She fell asleep afterward, dozing hard and long, cuddled into warm skin and secure in my arms.

Looking back, that episode was a plot twist, a critical moment.

hello, world

. . . a man, however well behaved
At best is only a monkey shaved!

W. S. GILBERT

Every day I pull on jeans or shorts and one of the assortment of tee shirts I own, all with loose necks and ring-around-the-collar. There's no point in dressing up because I know at some point I will get monkey footprints or food all over me. My hair is unbrushed—it will probably get routed through at the juncture between isolation and engagement, the times when I deliver a drink from a bottle or take her out to play. It's pointless to wear makeup, and jewelry is even more complicated; an earring could be pulled in exuberant play, dangling neck chains or pendants can catch big primate feet, and pinned-on ornaments scratch the monkey's belly as she digs to go into the bowels of my shirt, topside-down. If I could endure the cold, it would probably be best if I operated unencumbered by clothes, and I'm certain she'd be thrilled at the prospect of me naked like her. In any event, the home outfit is casual and messy.

For this reason and others, taking Ziggy out of the house became a hassle. Not only can you not go out frowzy-looking, you have to pack and prepare as if she were a baby—carrying diapers, wipes, toys, drinks, and because they eat most of the day, snacks. And if you're going to an important event, a change of clothes is recommended because you never know when you will get some type of sticky goo upon your person that will withstand all attempts at cleanup. By the end of the first summer we got her, however, I knew that sooner or later I'd have to jump into the outer world with her, and I might as well make a start. Luckily she was still small, and food footprints (much like spit-up stains on a mother's shirt) were the worst of my day.

It all came about one day after Jordan's Boys' Club baseball game. He wasn't much liked among team members because the majority of boys went to a rival school, and their territorial camaraderie was pretty well established. He told me he'd announced to his teammates that we'd gotten a monkey. In response, the others had said things like, "Sure, Campbell, and I've got a baby bear cub in my basement." One kid taunted, "I've got a giraffe in the closet in my room, too."

Not wanting to pass up the challenge, and unable to come up with a good reason not to, I asked Jordan if he'd like me to come to a baseball game and bring the monkey. I had helped him prepare for the season with several months of playing catch—I'd even given him his first black eye—but since Ziggy's arrival I'd been otherwise pre-occupied. Bringing Ziggy to the ball field, I thought, would prove to the boys who had taunted him that he did indeed have a monkey in the family.

My well-intentioned plan backfired. Instead of putting the spotlight on Jordan, I spent the entire ballgame walking around trying to escape the eager hands of little ones traipsing behind me. Ziggy and I would hear the pop of a fly ball, the groan of the losing team, and the rousing cheers from serious-minded parents urging their own kids to victory, and we longed to be *with* them. We wanted to see our batter-boy toe the dust, spit into his hands, and make his mark against his opponents—the creeps. Instead, we wound up fleeing the sticky fingers and pleading faces of youngster. The children, like ants at a picnic, chased us from the site, and we actually disturbed the game. Zig had grabbed all the attention and I missed Jordan's big play, a young man's milestone.

Later that evening I cornered him. He was getting ready for bed. "I'm sorry I missed your base hit," I told him while scratching the new red heat rash blossoming on my arm.

"Fine," he said, "fine."

I'm sure he thought no one had heard him.

SQUIRREL FOR A DAY

I don't make a habit of taking Ziggy out on the town. After all, I am a writer and being home writing is what I like to do best. For us, the "world" comes best in doses from newspapers, radio talk shows, or the Charlie Rose television program.

All wordsmiths, however, need to see the light of day in order to make some sense of the world—in order to hold a mirror up to society. (I write personal essay columns for a newspaper, so I know this. We try to capture the small details of life and expand on them to surprise, entertain, and educate. At least that's what the mission is.) Anyway, a short trip to Sears and Krogers—how bad could it be?

One day while I was waiting for a lawnmower at Sears, a bright-eyed, freckled kid of about six sighted Ziggy clinging to my arm. He asked if I had a squirrel.

"No, it's a monkey," I replied.

His eyes got as big as eggs sunny-side up. I took her closer for his inspection and invited him to touch her feet. He felt the soft palms, and following his "handshake" I told him about her tail and some of her habits. After listening to me intently the boy looked into my face and said with all earnestness, "Does she play cards?"

I looked down at the curious boy and said, "Not yet."

Ziggy and I always get a lot of outside attention. A simple errand is bottlenecked by throngs of curious observers. People from all walks of life are fascinated by primates, perhaps because they so closely resemble ourselves. Ziggy and I are magnets for little children and animal lovers; they gather in numbers larger than you would imagine. Short outings turn into long dissertations on why we have a monkey and what it is like to live with her. The good part is that it gives me the occasional opportunity to hype Helping Hands, pump up awareness for the disabled, or teach a session of monkey-talk.

I try to keep these visits quick, and milk them for humor—probably out of nervousness over her behavior. Not unlike your typical two-year-old, when you want Ziggy to behave, that is when she feigns being deaf. She will exit my shirt, climb up on my shoulder, and scratch my scalp in a pretend groom session. Lick, pick, lick, pick, lick, pick. I can't see her face, but I know she looks adorable. If she's feeling stressed, wants to show possession of me, or if she believes I am giving the other person too much of my attention, her gentle scalp scratches turn painful. Scratch, ouch, scratch, dig, scratch, arrgh! Her nails dig deeper and deeper into my skull. She knows that we are on display, and she also knows that I will wear the facade, smile, and take it.

In better times, when she is being socially civil, I like to tease, hand out the basic rap, and have some fun. Inevitably people will say she's cute, and I like to say "She takes after her daddy" and glance at my husband for effect. Mike never seems to mind being part of a joke or an affectionate farce. He will play along and mug like a chimp.

Most times "outing" with Zig is a considered decision on my part: If I have a lot of errands, if I think we might be surrounded by a large group of people, or if I need to buy groceries (Ziggy isn't allowed in Krogers although the manager said he hated to kick us out), I will leave Zig at home with one of the other members of my family.

A STAR IS BORN

Soon, word of Ziggy's arrival made us very popular. Our story had been covered by the local, regional, and state newspapers, and now the Channel 11 television crew was coming to tape a segment. I was tired and harried from the unscheduled full-blown housecleaning I'd undertaken in preparation of the unforgiving lens of the video camera. The boys got small lectures about combing their hair and brushing their teeth. Something else was going on, a sibling undercurrent that I wasn't privy to, because they were giving each other the silent treatment. Not unusual considering their ages, and because Ziggy was acting pretty hyper I didn't dwell on it.

Everything was finally ready for our television debut: The house was clean and I was in the kitchen cutting the last of the Arkansas summer fruits, when a compact car pulled into the driveway. No van, no crew of people, no lights, just one cameraman with a portable video unit and a small, dark-haired, young woman—about twenty-one—wearing a red close-fitting suit.

The "media" came in out of the late Arkansas sun looking like two who had found their mirage. The heat can do that to you. We gave them some time to adjust to the cool blue, white, and yellow rooms.

They relaxed and were charmed by Ziggy. Betsy, the TV reporter, was making faces at her, fascinated. I went into my pitch about the disabled. After all, the story wasn't simply about a human family raising a monkey. The real news story concerned the larger picture—the Helping Hands program and Ziggy's future role as an aide to a quadriplegic. Ziggy didn't know she was supposed to be the ambassador for this innovative program; she was just going to act like her mischievous self. She tossed toys off the dining room table and watched the humans pick them up. She jumped about on her froglike legs and paraded around. She climbed all over the cameraman and made flirty peeps in his ear, clinging to his arm with a viselike grip. Under the spell of strong monkey voodoo, the Channel 11 two were captivated. The family noticed all the signs. When the TV folks first arrived, they were assuredly cool and professional. One short hour later, they were both on the floor, competing for Ziggy's attention.

"Let me hold her," said the cameraman.

"It's my turn to talk to her," said the pretty girl. She held out a piece of watermelon to seal the deal. The juice ran into her sleeve, but she didn't seem to notice.

"Let's get her to run toward the camera," said the man, looking into his viewfinder. A task easier said than done. After what seemed like hours trying to get Ziggy to run toward the camera, he let her climb on board the camera itself. I held my breath and silently prayed that Ziggy would not eat the leather binding on the camera or play with the earrings of the compliant young woman.

I looked at my watch. Because Ziggy was literally a "short subject," it seemed like they were filming our calves, knees, and floor for hours. In fact, it had been four hours. Everyone was exhausted.

We waited a whole week to see our segment. We were told it would be on the ten o'clock news. Michael made popcorn for the television viewing as if it were a night at the movies. About halfway through the coverage of local shootings, politics, and weather, the kids began to get antsy.

"Maybe they're saving the best for last," I said.

I was anxious about seeing my latest surgery-altered face on TV. The previous winter–spring had been one of the lowest periods of my life. My last operation, in which pieces cut from the top of my skull had been used to rebuild my disintegrating jaw and chin line, had tested the limits of my endurance. I can still remember my doctor so thoughtlessly referring to me as "Andy Gump," a comic strip character I'd never seen, but who I knew could swallow his own teeth and jaw with just a pucker.

"Shut up," said Courtney to his brother, who'd been humming, "It's coming."

Well it came—and went. Our segment was about one minute long. What happened to all that taping?

My appearance on television was no more than a quick flash of some thick knees and a millisecond of my smiling mug, with Ziggy running around, willy-nilly. I had hoped for better. I had hoped my dissertation about this program and my plea for further consideration and help for the quadriplegics would have received a better showcase. *Ziggy stole the show again,* I thought. *Just like at Jordan's ballgame.*

As we would continue to find out, Ziggy grabbed the spotlight most of the time. She drew crowds. She was charming, comical, and so resembled a furry, endearing human.

A true star.

GO EAT WORMS

As we followed Zig's progress by using Spock's baby and child development guidelines, we knew that the "terrible twos" were just around the corner. We spent an inordinate amount of time waiting for the other shoe to drop. With my own children, the "twos" had been a time for obstinance, the requisite temper tantrum, and mood swings. A monkey approaches adolescence much the way a young child does—by acting agonistically toward any type of unwanted behavior and by getting destructive, noisy, and manipulative as a way to get what they want. The very best way to *cause* agonism was to take something away from Zig. Such actions would be met with a bite. Monkeys can bite. Let me say this again, *monkeys can bite.* They mouth and bite as a form of expression, in play, for domination, and in testing out every item they come in contact with. Ziggy had discovered her teeth. One minute she looked like a harmless little baby, sucking her thumb, making small noises and cooing sweetly. Then, bam!

During this period, her biting was subdued, nonaggressive but annoying. Courtney, Jordan, K-9, and then I, took it the most.

Mike got an occasional nip. I now know that was because my husband represented the so-called *alpha male*—the top ranking, the big Kahuna (there can be alpha-leading females, too).

I once made a funny family drawing of the boys and the dog and made X-marks where all their nips resided. This was a private family joke, something we compared and shared and knew she would grow out of. In fact, this is one of the habits Helping Hands expects families to discourage. I have been alerted, however, to the woes of the exotic pet trade where people unprepared for owning monkeys think they can gain control by giving monkeys a "good spanking." A good spanking is an oxymoron. There is no *good* spanking, especially with a monkey. They will only become more belligerent. I've learned from the experts at the USDA that if a person chooses to take his anger out in words or actions that abuse animals, it's the same as backing a beast into a corner; it's a challenge. A monkey would have to defend himself.

For preventive reasons, most Helping Hands monkeys have their front teeth removed. This may sound harsh, but in many states a monkey's bite can be reason for their autopsy—for rabies testing. Even though there is no real danger of rabies in monkeys that don't roam free or come in contact with rabid animals, they can still be put to death for rabies testing if they bite someone. To eliminate that possibility, Helping Hands recommends the removal of the front teeth. A factor we can live with, considering the alternative.

Ziggy exhibited other behaviors characteristic of adolescence: chewing, banging, and destroying things. We decided not to baby-proof the house because, one, we have a lot of stuff, and two, we don't give her full reign of the place. A local newspaper that did a story about Zig made a joke about her swinging off chandeliers.

Never in your life! Once we saw what she could do to an indestructible Fisher-Price plastic truck, that was her last wild ride around the house. She had eaten a hole through the thickest part. I keep it in her toy box as a keepsake and reminder.

The boys used to close her in their room and chase her about, and they had a blast doing it. Ziggy would rear up on two legs like a horse with a burr under its saddle, grab the nearest small object, tuck it under her arm, and run with it. One night when the whole family was lying on our king-sized bed, Jordan gave his empty Coke can to Zig. She drained the few remaining drops and took off, clutching it to her side like a football, running on those two huge feet. We thought about taking a photo of her with the Coke can and sending it to the advertisers, but we could never get it on film. The pictures were always a blur. So much for fame.

During this pre-adolescent time, her speed, curiosity, and possessiveness intensified every day. She took to rattling her cage door for any reason, and we had to change locks four times. In the beginning it was a simple slide mechanism. She reached around, slid the latch, and was out in a mere instant. Next we used coated wires. Mike would bend the wires carefully around the latch, and our Houdini would unravel them just the same. We advanced to a spring clip, but after hours of persistent fiddling, she figured out how to push open the clip. (For a lesson in determination, look to the capuchins.) We finally wound up with a combination lock and key. And she is so smart that I have seen her pushing toothpicks, a paper clip, twisted Kleenex tissue, and other odds and ends into the keyhole.

Another imposing character trait of capuchins is their speed. You will not "catch" a running monkey unless you are very clever, at least more clever and more unpredictable than the monkey. There is an amusing historical account that illustrates this very point. Apparently when Oliver Cromwell—the Lord Protector of England, Scotland, and Ireland—was a baby in 1599, his uncle kept a monkey at Hinchinbrooke. One day baby Oliver was snatched from his cradle by the monk, who scampered out of the window and onto the roof. He dangled the "Fortune of England" in his arms while the frantic family surrounded the house with mattresses. After a while the monkey tired of the game, trotted back on his own, and deposited the infant back into its cradle.

Ziggy, when freedom availed itself, took to playing a game of catch-me behind chairs so that when you crossed one way to grab her, she would dodge in the other direction, again and again like a large-motor peek-a-boo, only to escape running around and around like a clown with the cutting speed of a calf in a rodeo.

Around this time, too, Ziggy was grabbing for everything within reach. When she purloined an object, she would bang it to pieces or tear it apart. She once got a book off the shelf, ate the spine, and set about tearing out the pages one by one. If we let her, she would shred cardboard, boxes, and take great delight in either hammering inanimate objects or banging them against the cage walls. For attention, she will cage rattle—making the door bang—to let me know she's out of water or wants to play. I started giving her our junk mail and now she expects to get all superfluous mailings. Today this is her most favorite house-keeping habit. She licks the glue off envelopes and contest stickers, shreds certain kinds of papers but—mail-order merchants rejoice!—she does read and enjoy the occasional catalog, keeping it intact.

Extracting things is one of the habits readily *encouraged* for the "psychological well-being" of animals like Ziggy. This is government-industry jargon, and as an entity they have mastered the art of under-statement. People who know about primates—caregivers, zoo personnel, researchers, behaviorists—know that extracting is part and parcel to healthy, happy, captive animals. The effort of collecting food is just as important for a foraging animal as is sleep. It is, in other words, their work. This concept took a long time coming to issue at research institutes, and although it has become popular it is *still* only minimally instituted.

The U.S. Department of Agriculture mandates the minimum cage size for research animals, certain humane health regulations, and steps that owners must take to make their captive monkeys as content as possible. But monkeys are highly social and get bored easily, and psychological well-being means different things for different species. And unfortunately, you can legislate, but it is hard to know what goes on behind closed doors, especially with private facilities. The lives of primates confined to these facilities can be mighty sad.

Here at home we've made a game out of extraction. After Ziggy was weaned, she graduated to monkey chow, a high-protein food, heavy on nutrients, not unlike dog chow. Her diet consists mainly of chow, vegetables, fruits, and the occasional hard-boiled egg. I push nuts or raisins into peanut butter or bury a slice of banana in yogurt, and put the concoction into a small jar with a twist lid. I'll also wrap a small animal cracker into several folds of foil. Zoos typically use raisin boards: 2 x 4s with areas gouged out for hiding raisins. Anywhere you can hide food provides opportunity for extraction. Ziggy will even suck the contents out of grapes, raisins, corn, and peas, leaving the filmy shell. She will crack and shell raw peanuts, chip the shell off a hard-boiled egg, and scratch out a coconut. Making her feedings more like the wild foraging experience is always a treat for her, and it is beneficial for any captive animal's mental health.

THE PLAN IS NO PLAN

Most of the things we learned about Ziggy's behavior were unstudied initially. We didn't have any preconceptions about how Ziggy would act. And for the most part, I think that was for the better. Helping Hands just asked that we value her and raise her as part of a loving family—sharing and providing a foundation of love, understanding, and guidance. Just as families learn to cope, grow, and adapt with each transition a family member makes, we foster families know that part of the bargain is getting the monkeys through the tough parts.

My friend Paula, who is raising an industrious monkey named Emma, explains, "As Emma gets older, she learns to control her emotions more. That's why training is delayed until after socialization, giving the monkeys time to grow up. Our job is to go through all the ugly stuff." The "ugly stuff" is equivalent to the "terrible twos" in human children.

We knew that because all monkeys are individuals, what we read about primates didn't really matter; Ziggy would follow her own path. Of course, we spent a lot of time talking about new developments. Ziggy's pre-adolescent behavior was alternately aloof and eager to please, giving us a lot of material to puzzle out.

Monkeys live for the moment. Always moving ahead, humans don't take time to study faces and analyze every nuance of each person around us. Most of the time we're living on a kind of autopilot; then when we face down a catastrophe, time seems to stand still. Ziggy's growth, together with my recuperation from all the surgeries, was teaching me to appreciate the days when nothing much happened, when we could remember to watch her expressive face, compare notes, and try to decipher her body language.

Her vocalizations are limited to "uh-huh" for agreement, "hoo-hoo" for isolation, lip-smacking for conversation, "heh-heh" for alert-danger, crying for complaining or taking away, and screaming for being mad. Like anxious parents waiting for their child's first words, we watch for patterns that will help us interpret her utterings.

I ask Zig, "Do you love me?"

"Uh-huh," she intones.

"Do you want peanuts?" I say.

"Uh-huh," she replies. Sounds oddly similar.

But the noise when I come home from a short absence and she's greeting me is a composite of all of the sounds she's capable of, only higher in tone, squealish, and happy. It can't be mistaken for anything but joy. Her moods and expressions are all very subtle, and a half hour spent in front of her cage watching is never enough. Sometimes when you try to explain a look or a particular habit to others, you may not be able to define it but you know it when you see it.

Ziggy has this play face, a goofy look with a crooked smile, that tells us she wants to roll up into a ball, or sometimes she will attack her tail as if it has a life of its own and she acts as if she really has no control over whether it brushes her fur backward or comes up behind her head to tickle her ears. Sometimes the disembodied tail will curl around and stroke her face as if it were a strange appendage that just happened to be there looking for something to pet.

Friendly intent and approach with her is a complex gesture involving a grin, some eye closure, a small lowering of her eyebrows, headshaking, and vocalizing that sounds like a muffled "uh-huh-uh-huh-huh-huh." When anyone she deems important leaves the room, or is out of sight of her cage, she will plaintively call, "hoo-hoo-hoo." Such a sad bleating—it could never be defined as anything else.

Over time we became skilled at figuring out her signals and in gauging whether an encounter was aggressive or playful, depending upon her facial gestures, vocalizations, and posture. Behavior accompanied by the open-mouth, bared-teeth threat face was often aimed at new stuffed animals, the "underlings" in her cage world. Whenever she was given a new dolly—which is what we've taken to calling her stuffed menagerie—she would scratch out its eyes. We know that this is her way of removing confrontation.

Now she's even taken to removing a certain amount of stuffing from their innards, and some favorites have become a mere shell of their former selves. But she still carts around their empty carcasses.

Frans de Waal, a Dutch-born zoologist and ethologist affiliated with the Yerkes Regional Primate Research Center, tells the story of a capuchin monkey born in the Venezuelan jungle with partially paralyzed legs. Able to climb but not to jump, the monkey needed to be carried from tree to tree. According to observers, the group carried the infant more than usual for its age. De Waal says, "The bad news was that the infant consumed normal amounts of food. Having no exercise, it grew big and fat and became more and more of a burden." It seems the group's butterball was carried even at seventeen months old, when it mysteriously disappeared. It was never known if the "he's not heavy, he's my brother" mentality wore off, or if the fat infant was picked off as prey. As much as Ziggy treasures some of her dollies—personally, I'm inclined to believe it was the latter.

There is another commonplace phenomenon that always fascinates us—the *eye contact* notion. With capuchins, it might seem like a game, but it is not. Now that Ziggy was moving out of infancy, any eye-to-eye look was quickly averted. Even today, I can coax her into a stare down, but she will never face a stranger with a gaze. It's all about dominance and "saving face." And it is not exclusive to monkeys. Human behavior experts have determined that when people converse with someone of higher status, they tend to glance at him or her dartingly rather than hold a steady gaze. The higher status person doesn't look straight in the eyes of the lower status person either. Experts claim, "Powerful people do not monitor the less powerful."

There were other examples of Ziggy's behavior that seemed quizzical to us, the uninitiated. One was patting. I still do not quite get what patting is about, but it is obviously a comforting gesture. Zig likes to pat. She likes me to pat my chest, and she will catch my patting hand and stop it, and then take my hand and encourage it to resume patting. Curious.

Another interesting habit is anointing. If Ziggy is given something very citrusy like an orange slice or a grapefruit shell, or something with a strong odor, like an onion, she will rub it, squeeze it to extract the juice, and methodically use it on her feet first, then on her tail, and subsequently up the back of her body and over the head. In the wild the use of strong odors, including urine, in this way serves as a form of marking, perhaps as a deterrent for another species, or possibly as a kind of insect repellent. I have observed Ziggy pee on her hands and wipe it all over her fur, using her tail as a rag, an implement to distribute the wetness. Often we could facilitate the anointing by just giving her a bath in some essence or extract she isn't particularly taken with and then giving her an anointing source.

Lucky for us, her urine and feces are non-offensive smells—much less odorous than a cat box—and odoriferous in a sweet-sour smelling way only if ignored. I think this is mainly a result of her being primarily vegetarian. In the wild, capuchins will eat small birds, lizards, and various bugs, and although I could augment her diet with mealworms, June bugs, and crickets, I prefer to be the unambitious chef.

One other meal proclivity, though, is interesting to note. If you feed a capuchin a small meal, according to the nature of its constitution, you can expect it to defecate approximately fifteen to twenty minutes later. So if you are into timing events, this is another characteristic to add to the charts: a fifteen-minute digestive window.

EN FAMILIA

Jordan, then about ten years old, generally took the most time to interact with Ziggy, after me. He developed a game to test her tail balancing ability, at least until this game was replaced with a newer challenge: boxing. Ziggy had a stuffed Minnie Mouse doll and a piece of sheepskin she had brought with her from Disney World. Because these were her first instruments for attachment, they were important. So when Jordan started playing around with Minnie, the results, I thought, were surprising.

Minnie wore a red and white polka-dot skirt with a matching bow sewn into her head, just above her big plastic eyes. For some reason, the polka-dot bow drove Ziggy nuts. She was always trying to yank it off. Jordan figured he could have some fun with that. Standing the doll up on two legs, he pretended to hurl soft punches at Ziggy's middle, adding a cartoonish Minnie voice for good measure. Ziggy thought this was great fun and actually started to "box" back. Jordan continued to refine the matches, adding in more sound effects, making punching noises, and talking as he imagined a female boxing mouse might. I was a good ring-side participant and Ziggy seemed to realize that this game was a great way to get attention. She played along until, tired from the soft, stuffed punches, she would drop back. Then Jordan would pretend to make Minnie—defeated and spinning—"hit the dust." Ziggy would climb on top of her opponent and pull hard on the polka-dot bow in retaliation. Jordan would squeak (in Minnie talk) "Ow, ouch, oo-oo . . . don't do that, the doctor sewed that on." I may be anthropomorphizing when I say this, but I think Zig truly enjoyed playing the clown and became quite a good boxer in the process.

On the other hand, Courtney, an emerging teenager himself, did not interact too much with Ziggy. The monkey's hierarchy had changed, Courtney had fallen out of favor temporarily, and besides, life as a young teen had other things to offer.

Ana Perez Rivero, a foreign exchange student from the Canary Islands, Spain, came to live with us and would graduate from the local high school the following May. Ana was great company for me, as Jopie de Keizer, our foreign exchange daughter from Holland, had been. In a household with three men, Ana's presence gave Ziggy and me a more equal footing. Ana is a beauty, with wonderful dark brown hair and a lively wit. She assimilated herself quickly to this quirky household. She treated Ziggy with the utmost kindness, and Zig repaid her by pushing out her feathery red belly to be stroked every day.

At this point in time, Ziggy began eating everything in sight. Ana taught us a few Spanish words, including one particular phrase that applied to Ziggy and her rotund shape—"la gordita"—which, if I'm not mistaken, is exactly how it sounds, *the little fat one.*

As we were learning (and anyone entertaining the notion of raising a monkey needs to know), cute, cuddly monkey babies grow into screaming toddlers, which beget preteens and independence; then they grow into adolescents . . . and there's more to come.

the harpo factor

Love is an exploding cigar we willingly smoke.

LYNDA BARRY

Someone once said to me, "People who work with primates are special and different." It has taken me ten years to figure out what that means. Every primatologist I've met, and every scientist I've read about, such as Roger Fouts or Jane Goodall to mention two of the most widely known, will tell you in their writings how they've changed through working with primates. Most started in a roundabout way, doing a job or something they thought might be interesting, and then the primates endowed in their care began to leave an indelible stamp on their lives. Suddenly, nothing else they were doing was quite so important. The more their lives became entwined with their simian charges, the more they felt a need to be around primates and, in being around them, felt *and still feel* a need to nurture and protect them. Now Fouts and Goodall fund-raise and provide sanctuary for chimpanzees, but had you asked them in the first year of their careers, they probably would not have foreseen themselves as becoming spokespersons for their particular species of great ape.

P E O P L E ' S   F E E L I N G S   A B O U T   P R I M A T E S

Primatology is a passionate subject. Whether your interest grows out of a desire to observe their conduct, you have ecological concerns about depleting the species, or you are angry about cruelty to animals through research testing, it is pretty near impossible to be lukewarm to monkeys and their interactive role with humans. Controversial at times, maybe; boring? never. I have not yet met nor talked with anyone who has worked with, owned, or observed monkeys who did not have strong feelings for them and their unique character.

In the beginning, my desire to get a monkey was not altogether altruistic. When I signed on to be a foster parent for the Helping Hands program, I knew the monkey I raised would be trained to help a quadriplegic, but at the outset I was thinking of myself. In the aftermath of my illness and jaw surgeries, I was broken and had no earthly direction for industry, no sense of what I could do for work, no inkling what I could do to satisfy myself or feel useful. Psychologist Abraham Maslow, an original thinker who rejected behaviorism and psychoanalysis, saw man as a creative being striving for self-actualization—fulfillment of one's potential as an independent, functioning healthy person. I didn't feel particularly independent, I wasn't functioning as I had previously, and I was trying to work my way back to wellness.

I was too close to my own situation to figure out what my needs were or how to fulfill them. But when Ziggy came along, she was a baby. She needed me. She didn't care what I looked like, what my baggage was. She gave me a chance to start a new adventure. Learning about her became a quest. It was something for me to think about that was separate from myself, a reprieve from the constant wondering *Why me?*

There's no denying it: Ziggy affects my life in a big way. She's tacked her needs onto the bulletin board of my heart just as I had tacked up the letter of her announcement from Helping Hands so long ago when I integrated her into everything I did, blissfully ignorant of the sacrifices it would require. We read together, walk together, spend every waking minute together. She was and still is, a child.

Part of my impetus for writing this book was to correct some of the misconceptions people have about monkeys, particularly monkey ownership. One woman told me that all monkeys are evil because they bite. Another said that monkeys carry all the deadly viruses that make people sick. I've heard countless others say they'd like to own one, and wouldn't it be fun. Owning a boat would be fun, owning an ant farm is fun, owning a model home is fun. Owning a monkey is hard work.

If you're enamored with the idea of raising an exotic primate as a pet, ask yourself: Do you want to raise a child for the next forty years? Bimbo, a family pet capuchin in West Akron, Ohio, just died last summer at the ripe old age of forty-four! As his health faded, he became blind and the family had to chop up apples for him. His last drink was

Gatorade from a bowl because he was too weak to use a cup. A family pet capuchin requires a lifetime of care. If you have no network of support, no place to ask questions like Helping Hands, you are opening a Chinese fortune cookie with long and some-times confusing consequences. Confucious say, "Person who take primate must not have sulky kids or snarly spouses." In fact, some of the Helping Hands monkeys have lived in multiple homes because when families fall apart, face illness or death, or return to work, what happens to the monkey? Family life takes unanticipated turns and the monkey's lifestyle changes, too. But don't worry about the monkeys with Helping Hands; they usually go on to manipulate their new family. They adapt, find new loves, new lifestyles; trust me, they're fine.

Care must be taken to protect monkeys from common ailments, injuries, and illnesses—Ziggy can suffer from dehydration, and catch all the viral infections, colds, and diseases that people can. The USDA has heard stories of how families have lost monkeys due to carelessness or neglect—including cases of monkeys ingesting bleach, being injured by hazardous objects left out, and escaping out of doors. Some of these stories are painful to hear and can be likened to child abuse in humans. Thankfully, none of this is happening within the Helping Hands roster.

Your home must be stable. Stable enough to weather out the routine: I haven't had a real monkey-free vacation in ten years. Stable enough to tough out the extra costs and duties: special food, expensive vet visits, diapers, wipes and pads, weekly weight cards, washing linens and bedding and toys and food bowls and surrounding floors and walls and . . . you get the idea, and we haven't even gotten to adulthood. And it can't be stressed enough that every monkey experience will be different.

In our case, Ziggy has given us gifts that far outweigh the "costs" of raising her. She has allowed me to grow up. She has forced me to learn things about myself I never would have known otherwise. And she has added immense joy and wonder to a family that might have fallen apart if its mother had been left to wallow in her own self-pity. And my family advisor, Doreen, who works for Helping Hands as their "counselor around the clock" tells me that monkeys have helped out many people in mysterious ways.

I think because it requires so much of you; like a teacher expecting the best, you try to rise to your own expectations. I often tell my son, who owns more people skills than study habits, "Anyone can get into college. It's staying and living through the *process* that will ultimately make the difference in your life." And so it is with anything that really matters. So when I tell you my story, do not think it is the same for everyone. Life is different for each person. Just as raising a Great Dane puppy will not be anything like rearing a miniature poodle, so each monkey experience will be unique and different. And I'm not discounting other people's tales or holding mine up as the example. It just *is*.

I had an eye-opening experience when I met another foster family, the Kents. An older couple, they visited us once early on and brought with them their Helping Hands monkey, Kerrie, a little girl. The Kents had professional photographs taken of Kerrie, wearing a dress and mooning the camera! I laughed when I saw Kerrie because her coloring was so much darker than Zig; she was also thinner and possessed a much different character. (My competitive streak was revealed in my inner thoughts, which said: *My monkey is cuter than your monkey.*) The thing that struck me as fascinating was when Kerrie's father told me with a glum note of disillusion that Kerrie preferred his wife over him. It was true. Kerrie preferred the company of females in general. She wanted to climb into my arms and be stroked; she seemed very receptive to me.

I'd just begun to notice that as Ziggy entered adolescence, she showed a marked preference for being with men. I've since learned that about 2 percent of monkeys have a gender preference, and with this group, there is very little room for negotiation. Either they like men or they like women; there's not much room for in-between. That's why when Helping Hands places a monkey, the monkey's propensity is a key factor in the placement. They will not put a monkey that likes men into a predominantly female household. I should have made a mental note of that phenomenon, but I didn't want to believe that Ziggy would prefer to be with the men in my family more than with me. After all, I was the mother! Ziggy, however, went on to exert that influence with more and more intensity, and later it would become my undoing.

Interestingly, Ziggy's preference reverses when she is in heat. Normally, when a family member walks up to Ziggy's cage, she is eager to be petted, talked to, teased, and generally engaged. When her female clock chimes, however, look out. She will have nothing, I repeat, nothing, to do with men. She will hunch over in the back of the cage and ignore any attempts at communication from them. If they urge her to come out, she will come, but she will also squirm and make all attempts to escape and run to me. Sometimes, she will hide in the back of the cage and pull a towel over her head.

This PMS-like behavior is yet another common ground Ziggy and I share. And despite the uncomfortable feelings of rejection that my men experience in being rebuked, Ziggy has helped me in ways she'll never know. For while I continue to interact with the men in my family regardless of biological clock leanings, and though I still love them despite the sometimes antisocial or depressed feelings that wash over me (and are aimed at them), at least now they have a barometer with which to read our emotions. Thank you, Ziggy.

THE GREAT OUTDOORS

K-9, our Dalmatian, bounced around the room, rappelled off the wall and pounced on first one foot and then the other as in a skip, under my feet. There was only one thing that made her act like that—putting on my athletic shoes to go for a walk. In fact, we couldn't even say the word *walk* in front of that dog or she would squeal in modulated pitch, getting increasingly more desperate as if she would burst. We often called it the *w* word to keep her from going crazy altogether. I clicked on Ziggy's leash; she, too, was already jumping up and down.

Fall in the Ouachita Mountains is a magical time. The Great Magician turns the trees into screaming yellows, oranges, and reds. The colors serve as a cue to the locals to chop firewood for winter and head to the grill for the last summer corn and steaks. It also makes the walkers want to hit the streets, to take really long walks.

Walking has been part of my daily ritual for as long as I can remember. First I did it as a regimen to maintain weight-loss; then I reasoned, "We can't live in the woods and not experience them," and now, I do it because it keeps me fit and prevents me from getting depressed. The walks have been as regular and predictable as the certainty that every Monday dawns with a vengeance, no matter how many classic movies I squeeze in on Sunday night.

We walk two miles every day. It's either a square, round-the-block plan, or just one street with a hill we lovingly call "Big Bertha,"

up and down and back in just a tad over two miles. The first half of
the walk gets you pumped—it's all uphill—and the second half kind
of eases you back.

Ziggy's on a leash, but in all the years we've been walking she has
hit the ground only four or five times, pulling me bipedally like a
flat-footed majorette leading the parade. She prefers to ride. I often
feel that I'm the camel in a caravan when she sits in back of my head,
one leg on each side under my ears and mushes me on. Most of the
time, though, she will climb inside my shirt (I secretly think she is
intimidated by the woods) and hang off my left arm like a fireman
hugging a pole. I've often wondered if wearing an eight-pound
weight on the same arm every day year after year will one day make
me lopsided. I don't care.

K-9 is long gone now, but she was a trip to walk with. An experienced hunter, her kills tallied up. For every mile the primates
walked, K-9 would do ten, scouting out deep into the woods and
running to catch up just before we drifted out of eyesight. Fit and
stout from the exercise, she was wily too. Her method of capture
was astounding. She would throw herself into the base of a tree,
making it wiggle up on top. When the squirrels got sufficiently
alarmed, they would jump to the next tree, and in the process of
escaping, dip down in their flight. That is when K-9 would nail
them. I felt badly for the critters and used to admonish her daily, but
what good would it do?

Some days Ziggy will be freaked out by the woods' regular
inhabitants. We've seen box turtles, squirrels, rabbits, deer, wild turkey,
a quail hen and her chicks, an armadillo, and tarantulas in the fall. If
something is especially surprising, like a rustling in the leaves or evidence of some life form scampering away, she will cling tightly

enough to form a tourniquet on my arm; and if I don't make her physically ease up, my fingers will swell slightly and turn a tinge of blue. One time Zig turned a turtle over on its back, making her alert-sound, "heh-heh," which is reserved for all things strange and scary. Large black crows scream out their territorial boundaries and will sometimes beat their wings over our heads; owls hoo-hoo in the twilight and Ziggy will clutch me all the tighter. (Ziggy's manicures are a weekly priority for just this reason.)

In the summer, sweat will be beading down my midriff and Zig will occasionally stick her head back into my shirt and lick it off. Eventually, summer becomes the dog days of summer, pushing temperatures into the triple digits and we become one, melting into each other's arms. She will open her mouth like me, panting up the hill. Winter is better, and she is like a fur muff against my skin, warm and comforting, and I can feel her heart pounding next to mine. We've become an odds–on favorite for consistency because we walk in rain, sleet, extreme heat; you name it, we go. Believe it or not, it makes us hearty stock.

One particular day the dappled sun played hopscotch on the street, running patterns of light and dark across my face, and all of a sudden, Ziggy jumped up from her perch and nipped my cheek as if trying to exorcise the monster crossing my face. It didn't hurt much, and I petted her head to tell her I was all right. I knew instantly she'd imagined some demon that needed to be put in its place. Because I'm the only mother she's ever known and because jungle life has never factored into her existence, I find it fascinating when her protective instincts kick in. My home is her sanctuary, and the outdoors is a place to be watchful and wary. Does she realize that some of the animals inhabiting the woods are no bigger than herself?

Another day we wondered, as we got our bikes out of the garage, whether Zig would like the motion on the bike or if she would be afraid. We needn't have worried. She loved bicycling! On the downhill stretches, Ziggy's fur would part and blow softly in the wind and her long pink tongue would come out, licking at the breeze. You could tell she was happy. Even though the hills made my calves ache, we would go again and again. We soon nicknamed her "Biker Chick." She loves wheels—wheels that make our bikes go fast and wheels that she spins on the Matchbox cars she plays with in her cage. I didn't notice it until later, but the handlebar grips on my own bike have teeth marks, a reminder of our downhill days.

J U M P I N G O F F T H E C L I F F O F I N F A N C Y

As Ziggy moved into her physical prime, somewhere between two and three years old, some new developments arrived almost overnight. We saw evidence of her using combined motor actions. She would merge the forces of all four extremities and tail against her cage or other items. She appeared to be ambidextrous, able to use either hand for grasping, pulling, banging. And she performed some funny, unexplained, and extraordinary slips, blips, and behavioral conundrums of monkey feat—actions that I was moved to label the "Harpo factor," after the silent Marx brother who communicated with the aid of a horn and made us laugh with some very loose, demonstrative body language.

One evening while watching TV, Michael called me over to sit on the couch. (From his spot, he has the best view of the entire cage.) Ziggy had taken her precious Minnie, strung its body between the top uppermost bars, and twisted its neck like a corkscrew.

She then put her mouth over the doll's legs and went around and around in concentric circles like an acrobat girl in the circus, spinning by her teeth! She did it again and again; we were amazed.

Another day, we brought the monkey along on a visit to my mother's. She was housed in a fairly large animal carrier filled with her bedding and dollies. It was a roomy molded plastic affair and you could hear her thunk-thunking inside as she jumped up and down like a Mexican jumping bean. While we were engrossed in conversation, Ziggy diligently unscrewed the four bolts that held the lid on, popped out of the box with glee, and like lightning, came shooting out into my lap!

I had recently read a story about Andy, a big, adventurous capuchin male who was subjected to in-home observation with several different scientists over a period of sixteen years. Kathleen Rita Gibson, Andy's caregiver when he was around five and one-half years old, says that Andy's visual skills and attentiveness to fine details in his surroundings greatly exceeded that of his owners. For instance, considerable care was taken to ensure that Andy would not eat any poisonous mushrooms while he was outside, and Kathleen scoured the area looking for the deadly fungi just minutes before, but lo and behold, Andy found some specimens only a few millimeters wide and ate the tiny wonders before she realized it. Another time, she says, while Andy was sitting in his owner's lap, he suddenly shrieked, jumped into the garden, and hopped back onto her lap holding a decapitated snake about three to four inches long, which he proceeded to devour. She says, "I was unaware of the snake's presence and Andy jumped into my lap holding it in his hands." These examples are indicative of the swiftness that capuchins are capable of. They can marvel the most skeptical of owners.

About this time, too, Zig began playing tricks on K-9, whereas before she would have never spit in her general direction. One evening, I gave Ziggy some plain spaghetti. We got a chuckle watching her twirl it around. Then she took a couple strands and dangled them out of her cage, enticing the dog to come over in a "come hither" manner. The dog, in her open, dopey-headed way came trotting closer, flapping her tongue, delighted to get the free hand-out. No sooner had K-9 crossed Zig's territorial marker than we saw Ziggy's hand come out of the cage and slap K-9 right across the chops! After the smack, you would have thought the dog would learn a lesson, but she fell for that gag to the end of her years.

Two of the things Ziggy did for trickery she still does today. The first is a deceptive behavior. With her faculties at their zenith, she had great eyesight and keen hearing and, in fact, she had become such an adept watchdog that she would often beat the dog in issuing the harsh yawps that indicated someone was either driving up the hill to our house or walking on the street out front. Ziggy the "watch monkey" knows that I will always come in response to an alarm bark, and I noticed that she used it every once in a while when there was nothing in the vicinity. I would walk over to the cage and ask her, "What? What do you see?" Her fur would be standing out full and she would cock her head toward the bay window searching the street. Nothing. Sometimes she even continued the alert, barking in the minutes right after to convince me she had really been upset.

Other times she took advantage of the kids. She would climb inside their shirts, entering top-side down, making a U-turn at the belly button then kissing their nipples or bare skin. Sometimes she made chattering noises in their armpits, too. It tickled and her soft fur felt nice on their skin, so they liked it. Their father called them "marsupials." But Zig had ulterior motives. She figured out that if she wanted to check something out, or to run free, she could climb into their shirts, kiss their skin for a while, and when they had been lulled into compliance she would bolt out the bottom, effecting her escape. Michael, for the benefit of the kids, would yell, "Monkey alert, monkey alert," and make siren noises. The boys would scatter, assuming the football tackle stance and Zig would just pass right on through.

Most times when Ziggy escaped she would run to the kitchen and take the phone off the hook, or jump up in a corner. Nine times out of ten, I'd find her in the closet, hanging off the sleeves of my clothes. Today the shirt gambit is still played, and at olly-olly-oxen-free we can still find her in there, dangling off some garment.

In another sly maneuver of note, whenever anyone gets close enough to the cage to be examined by her prying fingers, Ziggy will perform a ritual pocket check. Ziggy steals objects out of pockets with the finesse of a master thief. While you are making a fuss over her feet or tail, she will be taking your credit card or pen to the back of the cage to squirrel it away. Zig will also turn her head and pretend to be looking at something important in the opposite direction when all she wishes to do is steal your glasses or gum. If keys turn up missing, we check the cage for stash.

Because of this hoarding, Ziggy earned another nickname, "Persistence," an apropos name because she never gives up when she wants something. We humans soon devised a trick of our own when we needed to retrieve an item that wound up in her cage and didn't want to open the doors to get it. We would initiate a trade. We'd point to the desired object and, at first, she would feign stupidity. But if we had something to offer, we could point to the item and she would fetch it in exchange for some food, usually a treat. Frans de Waal once said that he knows of no other monkey species with which you can strike a deal.

In his book, *Good Natured,* de Waal writes about some research he participated in where sharing between capuchins was observed. The researchers placed two monkeys in adjacent compartments of a test chamber with a mesh partition separating them. One of the two received a bowl of apple pieces for twenty minutes, and the other received cut-up cucumber. De Waal said that video footage of the experiment surprised many of his colleagues in that it showed caps handing, pushing, or throwing food through the mesh to their neighbor. De Waal goes on to say that this kind of exchange is simply unthinkable with most other primates. The Campbells are not surprised.

Zig mastered throwing, very early on, with an aim that is quite extraordinary. On cage cleaning days, she will throw feces out of her cage. Like a twisted Heloise, she thinks this method is quite helpful (she's giving me what she thinks I need). If you help yourself to a snack without an offering for her, she will pitch cups, lids, and thin dishes across the floor in front of you. Ice cream is her favorite mostly forbidden food, and if anyone has a bowl of it, she is sure to hurl some type of container from between the bars and it will unerringly roll across the room and land at the offender's feet. The folks at Helping Hands tell me any type of "lid-pitching" is discouraged—begging monkeys should not hold us hostage for food—especially when the monkeys are taught to get something for their paralyzed companions to eat. Besides people food is not always healthy for primates. This is something Zig and I have to work out. But, you know, I'm told the sign of a really smart monkey is when you hand them some object horizontally that can only be taken through the bars vertically, and they turn said object at a right angle for retrieval. For our Ziggy, that was a piece of cake!

Along with the observance of all things Harpo, at one time we thought about capitalizing on Ziggy's ability and its potential for making some serious money. At a family caucus, we decided we'd create a video and send it in to the television show *America's Funniest Home Videos*. After some consideration I came up with an amusing idea. We would build an entire Lego village in my mother's garage and film Ziggy knocking it down, similar to King Kong's vengeance wreaked against New York City. The kids were excited at the prospect and Michael thought it would keep everyone busy. The boys spent hours putting the metropolis together, using a mat that looked like road scenery and hundreds of Lego blocks and figures. They created a terrific cityscape, beautiful in its own miniature and eerie way. Then came the time to let loose our beast. We borrowed my brother's video recorder and positioned ourselves to shoot: Lights, camera, action!

Our film fantasy, however, turned into a farce. It was cold that day and the garage pavement was decidedly chilly. Not only did Ziggy *not* want to get down off her warm human perch, she wasn't even remotely interested in the play village. The boys repeatedly tried to talk her into the destruction, "Look, something you *can* take apart, monkey!" It was futile. She ran around the perimeters of the garage as if wanting to be anywhere but in the mean, monstrous town of make-believe. Later, after the boys disassembled the buildings, we shuffled home, a lot less richer for the effort. Like a psychic bunion, it ached to watch the television show, and we never turned it on again.

discipline, selectivity, and alex trebek

Of course we have free will. We have no choice.

I. B. SINGER

Before my age hit double digits, I remember sitting on the porch with my silent grandpa. He was jockey of a wooden swing that was suspended from the ceiling by chains, and the images formed from the clouds of pipe smoke he exhaled, plus the rhythmic eeking of the swing's "cheep-cheep," formed for me a clear and steady confirmation about what true peace was really like. I studied his demeanor and his look: He was frozen in time with his Czechoslovakian ways, pants that were short and strained at the inseam from trying to restrain a belly that had seen too many beers and shots. He wore

wildly patterned shirts and black shoes molded to his feet like a second skin.

He didn't speak English, not a word. But I knew my grandfather
loved me because he laughed when my cousin and I said, "Eh, Ga-
ram-pa" in our childish ways of imitating an exotic tongue. Still he
smiled and extended tender hands and gave us rough-bearded kisses
that smelled like burnt hemp mixed with almonds. And soon after
that period of time faded from my memories like childhood dreams,
I lost my instinct for reading other people. I became stupid with
naïveté, unable to decipher who was telling the truth or simply
pulling my leg. Later on in my teens, I was hit on by young men who
wanted only one thing. And still later, I was continually burned by
people I'd thought were my friends. In fact, that's one of the reasons
I married Michael: first, because I liked his version of me better than
I liked my own, and two, because I knew he would provide balance
for me, his yang to my yin. His skepticism to my naïveté. That's why
when Jordan started asking me about family traits for a school project
and Ziggy started to get choosy about people at the same time,
I blanked.

Apparently Jordan had first asked his father this question, and
Michael had said something very dad-like, such as, "I think you got
Mom's looks and my bad habits." He was playing with Ziggy at the
time; a moment earlier when he'd opened the cage, she had tried to
spring past him and I heard him say as he caught Ziggy's leg in mid-
air, "You get a piece of the monkey, you get the whole monkey." And
then Mike held the monkey up by the elbows and kissed her forehead.
She pretended to struggle and got more and more kisses. Ziggy had
grown so much that she had a hard time getting her yardstick-long
body into his sweatshirt and threading her Buddha belly through the

knit cuff on the neck of his shirt. But she burrowed in just the same and her hands came out and hugged his neck.

Jordan persisted. "What do you mean, 'bad habits'?"

"Well, not bad habits necessarily. More like natural abilities. Or talent. Like—don't be upset by this, Sport, but you can't draw. Me either. Courtney can draw and Mom is an artist. But us—nada."

"I *can* draw," Jordan protested.

"Okay, singing," said his father. "I can't carry a tune and you're no Elvis either. Tone deaf."

"I can *too* sing," replied Jordan.

"Listen," Mike said, "I'll sing my ditty. Then you." He was playing with the monkey girl, tickling her sides as she came out the bottom of his shirt. "Do your ears hang low, can you swing 'em to and fro . . . Can you tie 'em in a knot, can you tie 'em in a bow?" Upon hearing this, the dog began to squirm and showed her disapproval with a series of yowling noises. "See?" Mike said. "Case closed."

As innocuous as that story might sound, it says a lot about nature and nurture. I asked myself then—and a hundred times since—if parents always do right by their children's abilities, and how they can know if a child has missed the window of opportunity with music or art or sports.

Then, too, I wondered, what was Ziggy missing by not being with her own primate family? This question, or versions of it, plagued me for years before I finally came to terms with it. First of all, Ziggy was not conceived in South America; she was born in Florida. And she was one of us now, part of a relatively hairless family troop in comparison to her natural kin. Her status within the family was well established and her needs were taken care of. She had toys of higher learning, received plenty of stimulus, and was encouraged to have a relationship with her siblings.

She let us know she was happy by playing rolling ball games with her body and smiling and acting up. Did she miss the rain forest and trees and a life filled with itinerant moving? Because she didn't know the difference, I doubted whether it mattered. As much as I have romantic fantasies and dreams of how the world should be, it bears little relationship to the reality of the state of the world's environment and where it is leading us.

As far as Ziggy's life, I know it's great. And in respect to her life after me, she will do great again. I believe that monkeys have an inherent propensity to adapt. Simply put, *monkeys want to please the boss.* The larger, more complicated world issues aside, I can tell you that this miniature marriage survives; no, it thrives.

With regard to Jordan and his questions about "traits," Michael and I were careful to lay a string of self-confidence twined together with tales of our own family's legacy; it trails through the labyrinth of life so Jordan can retrace his steps out once he has slain the Minotaur, also known as biography. It worked for Theseus.

A FABLE

Understanding ourselves and our motives is not only important, it's vital. Recall the fable of the scorpion and the frog: Scorpion needs to cross the river, and he knows that Frog has the ability to get him across. Scorpion pleads and begs Frog for a ride across the river, crosses his heart and assures Frog of his safety. Finally convinced of Scorpion's sincerity, Frog sets out across the river with Scorpion riding on his back. Halfway across the river Scorpion stings Frog. As they both drown, Scorpion explains, "I couldn't help it; it's just in my nature."

Like the indefinable chemistry among humans, monkeys have definite feelings about whom they would like to spend their time with. They will get the object of affection in their crosshairs, and almost nothing can stop them from pursuing that person. At some point in Ziggy's development, it became her nature to want to have relationships with people she was drawn to. And she picked different types: smokers, a senior, and several TV personalities.

An interesting experiment occurred when Michael had a roomful of men over from his fantasy football league. His cronies comprised a cross-section of the men in the community, all sizes, shapes, and ages. It was a noisy, engaging exchange of camaraderie over football and beer. I found it fascinating to watch them vie for Ziggy's attention. With the ones she liked, she was open, engaging, and accepting of any tidbit or snack they offered. Some of the others left feeling slightly wounded that day because their affections were met with either a hunched-over indifference at the back of her cage, or a kind of half whining, half crying blather as if to say, "I don't wanna, I don't wanna."

It wasn't much different with the panoply of foreign exchange students who have passed through our realm. Michael and I were area representatives for six years for the Hot Springs, Malvern, and Benton area, and have witnessed some thirty-five students being processed through these communities. Ziggy has been greeted in French, Spanish, Dutch, German, Italian, Japanese, and Danish, and has heard English dialects from the Philippines and Australia. Her allure or ignorance of these people was as varied as her mood.

It was about this time that the concept of loving someone on the television came about, too. An avid *Jeopardy!* fan, Ziggy got a daily dose of Alex Trebek, and her admiration for him grew throughout the years. Now she is absolutely crazy over Charlie Rose, the late night talk-show host on PBS. Should we ever have the occasion to meet Mr. Rose, I am sure that Ziggy's intentions could manifest themselves in interesting and perhaps embarrassing ways.

The fact that Trebek, Rose, and a little later, Bob Vila, were two-dimensional television figures didn't lessen their appeal for her. When these personalities come on the screen, she will squeal with delight, sometimes thrust out her belly, and after a slight, spin-round tipsy ritual, she will settle down on top of a dolly, primed for the show, and suck her thumb. Occasionally she will answer their questions with a language of peeps, so we're sure that she's engaged.

R ED R OVER , R ED R OVER , L ET M ICHAEL C OME O VER

In animal societies where there is no such thing as lack of education, lack of opportunity, or inherited privilege, hierarchical structures are constantly changing. The shift in hierarchy comes about with the aid of important but subtle helpmates, mainly alliances. We of monkey families live through shifting power exchanges and alliances more than we realize. These alliances combine with subtle jealousies, which we don't always care to acknowledge at the time, and some-times, never.

I was so taken with Ziggy's attentiveness that my love made me dizzy—not unlike the time I had my first cigarette. So when Courtney would come sit by us and make a move to do something rather benign, like touch my chair or lean in close, and was bitten by Ziggy, I didn't realize it was jealousy. Courtney would react by screaming, and the monkey would scream in kind, and a strange screaming match would follow. Then I would chastise the monkey while tapping her nose hard. I'd tell myself, "She didn't mean it," or I'd try to find justification, like maybe he'd startled her or the tone of his voice annoyed her, when in fact, it was plain old jealousy.

Frans de Waal, famous ethologist, says, "In the primate order, the most widespread and best-developed collaboration is alliance formation, defined as two or more individuals banding together to defeat a third. For example, two male chimpanzees team up in order to overthrow the established ruler."

I only wish I had known about this concept earlier. Had I understood the inclination toward alliance and jealousy, and had I not viewed Ziggy's life through the filter of my own emotions (I even waited for her to torment herself with remorse when she hurt one of them), I could have been a smarter and better handler. For a few years Jordan suffered through times when he asked why Ziggy didn't like him. I tried to assure him that wasn't the case but the truth was I didn't have any answers. I would have liked to have told him the story of the scorpion and the frog and relate it to Ziggy: "It's just her nature."

Courtney, my older child, is an alpha of his own making and never let it get to him as much. As usual, I believed he had his own version of the story.

FOUR PERCENT BODY FAT (JUST GUESSING)

Monkeys are so fit. I've never seen a fat one, although we did try our best to make Zig our own family butterball—not consciously, mind you. It was just a way of buying her affection, or sometimes silence. Americans in general have a preoccupation with food as reward and happiness. We even equate food with love: The jingle "lovin' from the oven" comes to mind. So we overfeed our animals or feed them the wrong things, telling ourselves, "Oh, look, they want it so badly." How many dog owners have you seen who make drama out of their dog "begging"? Ziggy got more snacks by virtue of her being able to cage rattle, an extremely unnerving proclivity. This was her way of signalling the dumb humans that she'd inadvertently been excluded and, by giving her her due, one could correct the omission and silence the little beast.

Then enlightenment comes. Let's see, Ziggy weighs eight pounds. Hmm . . . if I give her half an apple, weighing about four ounces . . . that has to be a major overload to her system. A big Fuji is probably one-sixteenth of her weight! Might as well feed a bird a watermelon! When Helping Hands suggested we give her half a grape, honestly, I thought they were being stingy. Little did I know that we could make diabetics out of young monkeys. In addition, their unrefined, immature digestive systems aren't made to process chili-cheese corn chips and Claussen pickles. And if the preservatives and additives in processed foods give lab rats cancer, well, body weight-wise, monkeys aren't much bigger than the biggest test-case rodents.

It has been difficult altering her diet. We'd love to bribe her, cajole her, and make things all better with food. We tell ourselves that it's punitive to deny someone a treat. But then, that's our hang-up, not the monkey's. And as Helping Hands likes to remind me, monkeys need to mind their manners and they'd just as soon have dry shredded wheat or a hard-boiled egg, or even a cricket. Entire documentaries have been fashioned around the "termite on a stick" trick that chimpanzees have engineered in order to enrich their diets. Ziggy will likewise treat herself to the occasional insect when the opportunity presents itself. She can snatch flies, gnats, or other flying insects right out of the air and eat them before I've had a chance to say, "Ick."

She also likes to pick scabs, and because I always have an abundance of scratches from her scaling my body like Mount McKinley, there are plenty for her to pick at. It can be both embarrassing and tender, depending how you look at it. If performed in front of others, it can be her way of reinforcing alliance tendencies; almost as if she is saying, "This is my companion and I happily pick her skin." Along with other grooming services, scab-picking among monkeys provides comfort, ensures friendship, reinstitutes rank, and helps in reconciliation. One should feel honored for the privilege.

Another nasty habit she developed is hair pulling. This one was added to her repertoire of "retaliation tactics." If Ziggy misinterprets your intentions or doesn't want to pass up the opportunity to cause a little mischief, or if you're too near the cage and diddling around, she will grab a hunk of your hair. It will happen so fast, you barely have time to react. You have to understand her territorial boundaries encompass not only the cage but an invisible line some eighteen inches around the cage, which would be the length of her tail or an outstretched arm. Thankfully, her hair tugs are usually more annoying than painful.

In a different vein, I have a story to relate about a person who was deliberately cruel to animals. Someone once told me about a serviceman stationed in the Middle East somewhere, who got a monkey (probably a macaque) for a pet and chained it to his locker. One of the men in the barracks hated monkeys and every day when he passed the critter he would call it names or speak in a disparaging manner. The monkey would strain at its leash trying to retaliate but the recruit always remained just out of reach. One day, the monkey had worried the clasp on his restraint and waited for the mean recruit to come by. When the soldier predictably performed his discourteous harangue, the monkey attacked. I'm told it took four men to get the avenging monkey off his face, and it was not a pretty sight. Remember this cautionary tale if you ever think for a moment about tormenting a primate or witness someone else involved in such behavior. You heard it here.

monkey smarts

*Peppe is getting so much smarter. It wasn't so
long ago that he used to rip up the* TV Guide, *but now he has
graduated to ripping up the* Reader's Digest.

ANN IMPERATORE
discussing Peppe, a capuchin monkey

There's an old story: Stick a dozen monkeys into a locked room with
keyboards and computers for each, and in about seven years, they will
have written all the classics. Personally, I think Ziggy would rather
tear up the classics than write them, but she exhibits ingenuity and
has, at times, lived up to the nickname Houdini. Remember? She
progressed from a cage door with a slide lock (which was a piece of
cake to escape), to a tied-up braiding technique (her watchful manner gave its facility away), to a clip system (no problem for an animal
with opposing thumbs and stick-to-itiveness), to a key lock (she's

tried to stick objects into the keyhole ranging from Popsicle sticks to twisted Kleenex to paper clips).

Early on, there were indications that we were dealing with a thinking, sentient creature. Ziggy had been with us only a few months when my friend Sandy Lang came over to work on a sorority scrapbook. She and Ziggy hit it off right away. Ziggy, still an infant at the time, made sweet squeaky noises aimed at Sandy, and cocked her head coyly when Sandy cooed back. My friend had brought along her camera. She called Ziggy's name and asked her to look up, and Ziggy put on a cute, ¾-profile for the picture. The instant flash went off, lighting up her face and bouncing its reflection off her eyes. When Sandy readied herself for another photograph, the monkey shook her head, averted her gaze, and covered her eyes with her hands! We thought, *How smart, how clever, how cute,* despite the fact that she would have eaten the paper from our cupcakes in order to partake of the crumbs (something she had done just the day before).

Studies about monkeys and intelligence have revealed some surprising things. A team of Harvard researchers have even shown that wild rhesus monkeys can add. The scientists based their conclusion on the assumption that individuals—whether human or simian—look longer at something that is out of kilter or unexpected. The monkeys observed as researchers placed one eggplant, then a second, behind a screen. When the screen was raised, the monkeys saw two vegetables and quickly lost interest. When the test was repeated, a team member performed an out-of-sight, sleight-of-hand, tucking one of the two eggplants into a hidden pocket. When the screen was raised a second time, the monkeys looked at the results significantly longer, apparently confused. The scientists concluded from their reactions that the monkeys understood that $1 + 1$ does not equal 1. This particular test drew skepticism from others who claimed the methods were sloppy, but the truth remains: Few researchers doubt that monkeys can understand numbers. Given the choice of taking treats from a bucket containing four tidbits or a bucket holding only one, the monkeys unfailingly choose the former.

Sarah Boysen of Ohio State University has shown that chimpanzees can match groups of up to three objects with a placard showing the number of objects. Boysen claims that chimps can even learn the concept of zero. Still other studies, completed by other researchers, have proven that both chimps and monkeys have been taught to understand fractions. Boysen says of numerical ability, ". . . it is not unique to humans."

People always ask me how smart Ziggy is, expecting me to compare her ability to a child's—something they can understand. In his book *Peacemaking Among Primates,* Frans de Waal takes exception to this method of measurement, stating that the calculated power games of adult male chimpanzees and the mediation skills displayed by adult females suggest that their preoccupation and social awareness are more closely comparable to *adult* men and women, not children. De Waal describes families that have raised both ape and child together: "They play the same sort of games (king of the hill, blindman's bluff, tickling matches) and show the same carefree attitude. Their sense of fun, communication, and even taste in television programs match perfectly. When Winthrop and Luella Kellogg took hundreds of standard measures on the growth and development of their son, Donald, and a female chimpanzee, Gua, they found the ape doing better than the boy. She ate with a spoon, drank from a glass, and announced her bladder needs (by slapping her genitals with her hands) at an earlier age. Even in word comprehension and many of the intelligence tests, Gua was ahead of Donald."

I know Ziggy is smart but I have not conducted intelligence tests per se. My friend Paula Puckett, foster mom to Emma, a highly adaptive female capuchin, has done some interesting experimentation. Like most Helping Hands foster parents, Paula believes that Emma understands language. Paula's father, however, didn't believe Emma had this ability. To prove her conviction, Paula put a grape in her pants pocket and said to her monkey, "Emma, I have a treat." Emma immediately went for a shirt pocket—choosing the wrong one. When Paula told Emma to look in the other pocket, the monkey did, locating her surprise. Thereafter, Paula's father never disputed the claim that monkeys could learn to understand language.

Paula has also taught Emma to recognize colors. She believes this type of training provides good stimulation for Emma. It's not unlike what mothers do to engage their energetic preschoolers. And the best way to teach a child—or an imp—is to make a game of it. Paula bought big colored plastic Easter eggs, which Emma couldn't open at that time. She let Emma watch her put a treat inside each egg. Then she asked Emma to fetch a particular colored egg and place it in her hand. When Emma selected correctly, Paula would open the egg and give her the treat, reinforcing the lesson. She eventually taught her monkey how to distinguish between the colors blue, orange, red, and green. Using this technique, Paula has even taught Emma the difference between a fork and a spoon.

I try to steer Ziggy toward more artistic pursuits. Helping Hands has a picnic and small convention for foster families in Boston every other year, but for one reason or another, Zig and I have not yet been able to attend. One of the highlights of the convention is that they auction off "monkey paintings." I've always wanted to see the other artists' work. My Zig is a whiz with chalk. I will give her some color—she's partial to purple—and she will scribble on the 3 x 5-inch index cards I provide until she tires of the small canvas and continues her masterpieces on the walls of her cage.

Art spills over into her life. The other day my prodigy sat on a small table while I cleaned her cage and, to my surprise, she took a felt-tip pen from my memo box and drew a design on an envelope for Ink Jet Products in Ohio. I'll be needing more fluid for my printer soon, but I'm loath to part with the envelope.

On Sundays, Ziggy helps my husband make his picks for the football pools, penciling in her choice. Michael has done an adequate job with his own regular picks, but on the "Wally pool"—the one Ziggy helps him with—he's done better!

Teaching primates isn't restricted to scientists and foster families. I recently read a historical account that I find truly fascinating. The story is about two women, one named Meg and the other, the story's author, Rose Macaulay. It's dated 1956. It isn't clear how the women came to acquire an ape, but the story is that Rose wanted to teach the ape to drive. Apparently Rose felt that driving was a "crucial test of brain," and wanted to prove the ape could handle it.

Rose writes that the ape had a tendency to speed, pressing on the accelerator with all its might, and was prone to continuously honk the horn, which she says, "it enjoyed greatly." Rose goes on to say she forbade the primate to honk, unless there was actually something *in the road in front of it*. The ape did try to follow her instructions, she claims, although about the horn-blowing notion, "it frowned and ground its teeth," and she soon realized the ape would be a relentless, hooting driver. Rose also writes that the postman and the newspaper boy, who often traveled by bicycle, were alarmed by the ape's style of driving. The townspeople talked about it too, but she assured them that everything was "under control."

One day the ape got into a car alone. The vehicle happened to be standing in the drive with the key inside. The ape started the car, then drove through the gate and onto a field path. Some horn blaring was made at the gardener, who at the time was pushing a wheelbarrow full of leaves. The gardener had only seconds to leap aside as the car hit the wheelbarrow. Meg and Rose were returning from a walk when they caught sight of the gardener shaking a stick at the ape. The ape was blaring the horn and "gibbering at the gardener, who did not dare to get very near it."

The ape passed Rose's "crucial test of brain," but at a significant cost to the women, who had to pay for the wheelbarrow as well as the damage to the car. As ingenious as Ziggy can be, she won't be signing up for driving lessons any time soon.

M E M O R Y ,   T H E   M O T H E R   O F   W I S D O M

I've heard it said that monkeys and apes have 100 percent recall. That statement may be true, but it needs some refining. Although non-human primates may remember everything they're taught, they may not always want to *behave* as they've been taught—a fine distinction.

One heartwrenching story about primates and memory concerns Roger Fouts and his association with Booee, a chimpanzee that had learned American Sign Language as part of a research program Fouts had worked on. After leaving that program, Booee became a subject of biomedical research. He lived in the Laboratory for Experimental Medicine and Surgery in Primates (LEMSIP) at New York University.

In 1995, ABC's *20/20* produced a segment about the morality of bio-medical experiments on animals. They asked Fouts if he'd be willing to be reunited with Booee on television.

Fouts agonized over the decision. He'd had bad feelings about Booee's transfer, along with some other chimps, back in 1982, but he'd been powerless to do anything about it. He was dogged by their history together and what they'd meant to him and his family. He didn't know if he could face Booee again, especially in a laboratory setting. He finally agreed. Commentator Hugh Downs, Roger Fouts, and all of viewing America wondered if Booee would remember his previous life and teachings after thirteen years of restricted captivity and laboratory conditions. (In the name of research, Booee had been infected with hepatitis C, a virus that causes progressive liver disease. He was now twenty-seven years old.)

I can vividly remember watching that *20/20* segment; I felt Roger's pain and helplessness as he prepared for the reunion. As Roger entered the lab and donned a white coat and booties, I realized I'd been holding my breath. The camera seemed to be moving in slow motion. What would Roger see? Was Booee a different kind of beast? It was killing me. I'm sure viewers across America were on the edges of their seats. Then . . . Yes! Booee not only knew Roger but seemed thrilled to see him. He signed a nickname coined for Roger long ago that even Roger had forgotten: "Rodg." It was done with a flick of a finger off the ear. Booee remembered his friend, and he wanted to talk.

I watched that reunion and I cried. I cried for Roger Fouts, knowing the anguish he must have been going through. I cried for Booee, and for all the Booees in research everywhere. I cry in relating this story. Yes, the apes do remember. After thirteen long years of being manipulated by men of science, Booee not only remembered Roger, but also fell back into his old pattern from happier days— signing, asking for treats, and grooming.

Booee's story had a happy ending. The *20/20* segment generated such an outpouring of compassion that Booee and eight other adult chimpanzees were retired from LEMSIP. They live at the Wildlife Waystation in California and seem to be content in their "retirement home" with its sunlit rooms, toys, and memories of a better day.

BUTTERFLY DREAMS

A Chinese philosopher slept and dreamt. He dreamed he was a butterfly dreaming that he was a man. When he awoke from the dream, he was not sure whether he was still the butterfly dreaming he was a man, or a man who had dreamt he was a butterfly.

What do monkeys dream? Do they dream butterfly dreams? Or do they think they're humans? Much is made of apes and monkeys looking into mirrors. In the past, scientists set mirrors before apes and monkeys and discovered that the apes eventually came to regard the image as their own: Using it to erase a paint marking on their forehead, checking their teeth or genitals, or otherwise associating reflection with self. Some scientists claim that this trait is unique to humans, orangutans, and chimpanzees, and that because they exhibit consciousness and are capable of introspection, they are smarter than other species.

Ziggy's cage sits in front of a mirrored wall. I chose this spot first, because it is an easy surface to wipe clean and, second, I felt it would provide stimulation for her. Her reaction to the image in the looking glass can be best described as *confusing*. There are times it appears she is making aggressive, open mouth faces at the monkey in the mirror, as if to say, "That monkey is a bad girl." When it is dusk or nighttime, she will run to the uppermost corner of the cage, look into the reflection, and hold perfectly still. What this means I cannot tell. At other times, she appears to hold stare-down contests with her reflection. When confronted with the mirror up close, she will touch her reflection and display a variety of looks, mostly confrontational, some just curious. Sometimes, she simply talks, a chatty, lip-smacking kind of talk. Perhaps she is practicing conversation and conviviality, much like speakers practice speeches in front of a mirror. Or maybe she has conversations with her reflection as a child talks to her dolls, a play-pretend scenario of social tea and crumpets.

Can this be interpreted as self-awareness? Or does her possible *lack* of self-awareness represent a form of mindlessness in scientific terms?

Frans de Waal writes about a monkey named Azuit, a long-tailed macaque who plays with mirrors all the time. De Waal says that Azuit has learned to use the mirrors to his advantage, to see what humans or dogs are doing behind his back. To my knowledge, Ziggy has not devised such a crafty use for her mirror, but I often wonder whether she uses the reflection when she is alone as I used an imaginary playmate as a fanciful child. I wouldn't be surprised.

In the wild, monkeys leap great distances and catch themselves by the merest branch. What looks like complicated choreography is rendered with complete ease. They are neither panting nor do they appear uncertain of their physical capabilities. In this instance, their perception of themselves is inherently acute. Ziggy has leapt off a ladder and landed on the tops of my shoulders without disturbing so much as a hair on my head. Upon her landing, I feel a quick adjustment of pressure through the tension on her legs as they meet my body, but no pain or discomfort. Is this not self-aware?

And how do you answer the "self-awareness" question with respect to the unique life and social arrangements of a species like the macaques? Their entire world is ruled by a specific and clearly defined family tree of respect, rank position, and sociability, their every move a reflection of where they are located on the branches of hierarchy, within a confusing and evolving kinship network. One could say they are the arbiters of a convoluted *Who's Who* of social registry, not just for themselves but for their entire troop, knowing full well who inhabits the upper rung and whom they would like to pair their infants with. How could this be possible without some form of innate recognition of self and of their place in the world?

Regardless of scientific opinion and theories of self, I have no doubt that Ziggy knows where she belongs in the scheme of our own family: at the center, where else?

C A N   W E   T A L K ?

I find it amusing when the learned among us, psychologists and sociologists mainly, elevate humans above our primate counterparts by virtue of our capacity for speech. For many of the adults I know, believe me, speech is not an asset, and as far as me making my wishes known to Ziggy or vice versa, I don't see much difference. When it comes to recognizing her whistles, squeaks, chortles, and beeps—truly, I have no real dilemma understanding what she is trying to convey. Yes, monkeys can be unpredictable, but after years of reading her face there is hardly anything she can do that doesn't send me some kind of signal. Eyes opening wide, the goofy smile, the wary crooked look, and the face of reconciliation, these and hundreds of others send clear-cut messages like, "I'm interested in playing. . . .

Getting your bagel makes me happy. . . . Sorry, sorry, sorry. . . . I don't want to act out, but you're pushing me," and so on.

Some gorillas enjoy dishing dirt as much as the most meddlesome human gossips. A Stanford University primatologist, Robert M. Sapolsky, has written about Koko, the gorilla who learned sign language. Sapolsky says, "After watching one of her human teachers argue with his girlfriend, Koko couldn't help telling another human teacher about it."

Sapolsky also believes that baboons are voyeurs who love to watch other baboons fight. Although some humans may blush over being caught spreading gossip, a baboon will jostle for position in order to get a better view of an interesting tension playing itself out between haggling troop-mates.

This brings to mind a remarkable story I read in an anthology called *Magnificent Menagerie* by Lucinda Lambton. Apparently, the range of simian intelligence is as varied as that of humans, and the primate in this story possessed a brilliance to rival many humans.

Mr. Wide was a railwayman in Uitenhage, South Africa, in the early twentieth century. Poor Mr. Wide, who was in charge of switching the tracks and other stationhouse obligations, had lost *both* his lower legs. To assist him, Wide trained a baboon he named Jack to work the lever of the signals and carry out various other duties, such as pumping water, gardening, and locking the door. Jack also learned to push Wide back and forth on a trolley that had to be put on the rails by the baboon.

On one occasion when Wide had injured his arm, Jack took over all his signal-changing duties. (There is a picture to document this scenario; it's of Jack carrying some artifact of work and Mr. Wide in railway hat and coat, leaning against the wall of the stationhouse.)

Certain passengers objected initially to having a baboon tend to the signal changing, but a reliable witness said, "Jack knew every one of the various signals and which lever to pull as well as his master himself." It was also common knowledge that Jack had never failed during his many years of work. Indeed, some passengers felt that Jack had, on several occasions, acted in a manner simply astounding for a nonhuman primate. On one particular occasion, Jack defended Wide in a quarrel. Another time, he drove off a foreman by beating him with a dirty coal sack.

Skeptics may find this story hard to believe, but it has been heavily documented. An account filed in the Port Elizabeth Museum's collection contains an interview with Wide, as well as written statements of twenty-five witnesses. A final note adds: Mr. Wide and Jack were extremely close, a relationship expressed by mutual grooming.

THE 100TH MONKEY PHENOMENON

There is something transcendental and magical about evolution and learned consequences, and the story of the 100th monkey phenomenon illustrates it nicely.

There is only one monkey species found in Japan, on several different islands, the Japanese macaque, sometimes informally called the snow macaque. A beautiful thick-furred creature, it is the only primate genus able to withstand a cold, snowy winter and the near-freezing temperatures of the region. In some parts of its range, the macaque spends long periods of time immersed up to its neck, thawing in the hot thermal pools—looking every bit the tourist. Social groups of up to forty individuals live together, usually led by an older male. Their family relationships are important because females remain in close association with their mothers until they die, and males stay with their kin until adolescence.

In order to better observe these highly ordered creatures—and to keep them from raiding the farm lands—in 1952 and 1953, the monkeys were moved to the outlying beach regions of the islands. Primatologists and other researchers assisted the provision of the monkey troops by feeding them bundles of wheat and sweet potatoes (a favorite food). The food was left out in the open areas on the beach front, on the sand. A scientist named Lyall Watson, along with five other Japanese primatologists, wrote numerous articles on these macaques and a film was made in 1983 documenting their research findings about this particular relocation and its consequences.

One day a youngster, an eighteen-month-old female named Imo, was being observed on Koshima Island. She picked several sweet potatoes from the pile, took them to water's edge, and washed the sand and grit off the edible tuber. She then demonstrated the washing technique to her mother and a few other playmates. In time, the younger generation taught the older monkeys this ritual, and, according to Watson, by 1958 *all the juveniles* on Koshima were washing their sweet potatoes. The only adult washers were those who had learned this behavior from the children.

The mere fact of the monkeys washing the sand from their food is only part of the story. The really fascinating part is that at some point in time—Watson speculates it was with the 100th monkey—one further convert was added to the troop in the usual way. Then the magical happened. Watson says, ". . . the addition of the 100th monkey apparently carried the number across some sort of threshold, pushing it through a kind of critical mass because by the evening, almost everyone was doing it. Not only that, but the habit

seems to have jumped natural barriers and to have appeared sponta-
neously, like glycerin crystals in sealed lab jars, in colonies on other
islands, and on the mainland in a troop in Takasakijama." In other
words, the group consciousness of food washing developed in a slow
and gradual manner, until a groundswell of universal awareness took
place and created a sudden jumping of all natural boundaries.

Pretty amazing stuff this washing and water business. Some things
are not easily explained and I revel in that knowledge. Albert Einstein
once wrote, "The most beautiful thing we can experience is the mysterious. It is the source of all true art and science."

I suppose that's how jokes like the one about monkeys writing
the classics came to be. We revel in the idea of mystery and find pleasure in the perplexity of "what ifs." These are possibilities that seem
odd and funny and yet, every once in a while I catch Ziggy pressing
the letters on my computer keyboard, and I pause to wonder. . . .

a blond, tattered dolly

Monkeys make terrible pets because they're like human children,
and human children make terrible pets.

JIM WHITE,
foster parent of Cassie

Every day is monkey business; it never ends. First thing when I get up in the morning, I say hello to the sleeping primate tucked under the covers. That triggers a somewhat alert posture that sets me into gear, and I get a children's "animal" chewable vitamin with extra vitamin C and beta carotene and present it to her smooth, little brown fingers. Next I create a baby bottle mixture with a 1:10 ratio of juice to water or fill a bottle attached to her cage with fresh clean water. Then I cut a very small piece of whatever fruit is in season, make a soak of monkey chow in a small amount of liquid, and pop in a nut or two. Only then can I blend myself a drink, take the garbage out, pick up the newspaper, or get my own breakfast. Monkeys thrive on routine just as children and dogs do; sometimes, met by an unexpected adventure, their little thighs will shiver and they need to be reassured that things will be all right, nothing bad is going to happen.

The fact that monkeys will go back to sleep and will sometimes sleep for up to twelve hours, allows me a larger share of day-readying freedom. Still, she is my first appointment of the day; because I claim a downright passionate regard for the species' welfare in general, and for Ziggy especially, I think about her the majority of every day. It was different with the boys when they were young. Because I never got operating instructions with them, I allowed them to be very independent. They were always responsible for dressing themselves in the morning, getting their own breakfast, and moving out into the day. The fact that the school bus stopped in front of our house from kindergarten through graduation helped tremendously. But back to my point and where it was going: the passion with primates and why I lament when people get things wrong or say dumb things about them.

S. O. P.

For those of us who raise children or animals, we are fooling ourselves if we picture smooth, endless days of standard operating procedures ahead. I suggest keeping a journal about your experiences and feelings to remind yourself about the day your infant spit up on your Armani suit or the time you felt frustrated changing a diaper at O'Hare airport or the weekend respite that was canceled because of a childhood illness at home. Remember, too, the afternoon your child gave you a rock and you thought it was the best gift in the world, or the time he matched socks by tying them in a knot.

In my newspaper column and my journal, I have written about the shock of seeing my Dally [Dalmatian] vomit asphalt on the salmon-colored carpet, the time the cat mistook my bean bag chair for a litterbox, and the night I sat up because I thought Ziggy would die from licking Neosporin off a cut. On the other hand, I have an entry reminding me how great it felt when our Norwegian elkhound, Shana, pushed open the bedroom door several steps ahead of her visiting master and jumped on the bed to greet me when I was in a cast, and the time my sweet old Irish Setter, Thirsty, tried to nurse a litter of kittens. Getting a truer picture of the days—all the days— helps us to appreciate both the quiet times and the frantic times with equal weight. That much I've learned. The uninspired day on the calendar has become my balm for the rest.

The idea of keeping track of time, personal feelings, and changes in a journal, now that I look back on it, makes all the sense in the world. It allows us the chance for mindfulness and enables us to stay ahead of the game. Staying ahead of the game would become a real necessity for both me and my family because there were other forces to be explored with Ziggy's coming of age: sexuality and aggression. These are the two areas of contention most monkey handlers will agree they deal with most often. The power and sustained energy of these life passages means it helps to have a network of aid (thank you, Helping Hands), or at least some way of acquiring sage advice.

If you think that an animal has no sex life, I hope your cave is comfortable, for one would have to have been living in a cave to think we are the only species with sexual drives and needs. Perhaps, like me, you witnessed sexual behavior in animals early on. (If you grew up on a farm, that's a given.) I'll never forget my visits to my friend Pamela Anderson's house when I was a junior in high school. The Andersons had a large boxer of whom they were very proud. I like dogs, but this huge, slobbering beast had developed a chemistry bond with me that was pretty unnerving. He would assault my crotch with his snout, and then wrap his trembling flanks around my leg and hump it as if I were the boxer of his dreams. The animal— I must have repressed memory of his name—always had to be contained when I visited my friend. I would even call ahead in order to preserve my dignity, not to mention my outfit.

Although it was unsettling to be on the receiving end of his displays, I wasn't alarmed. I felt then as I do now: It was all very natural. Dogs act on their immediate needs, their inchoate hungers, and we have to love them, warts and all.

Ziggy's first bout with sexuality took on a much subtler comportment. I would come to refer to it as *chemistry,* and I am continually amazed at who she chooses to have chemistry "with." Several years ago I studied graphology with a Catholic priest, Father Tony Becker. A congenial and altogether pleasant man, Father Tony reminded me of Santa Claus with his rosy cheeks, white hair, and commanding but benevolent presence. One evening while the Father was at our home for dinner, Ziggy glommed onto his arm and spoke the high, squeaky words of love. It took more than a short while to pry her off his arm. I silently thanked the munificent presence above, because we knew what she might "normally" do if left untended. If Ziggy had a thing for someone, she would climb up their arm and position her stomach over their face, wrapping both arms and legs around their head in a position resembling a coonskin hat worn as a catcher's mask.

Another incident occured when Helping Hands asked if I would meet with a potential foster family, as they were wont to do several times over the years. My family always likes to play "show and tell" with prospective parents and it's a super special feeling when it works out and they become foster parents. This particular visit was with the Browns, Patti and Marc and their two boys, Chris and Luke. They had a new home in this region and we welcomed their visit. All went well. Ziggy was a good girl and a willing host. But there was one awkward moment when Ziggy decided that Marc was an ideal object for her affection and mounted his face. This was the first time Ziggy had ever "hugged" someone outside the family and I apologized profusely. Marc was a complete gentleman. He continued to talk as if nothing was amiss, and after a photograph and a fair amount of time, Zig was taken back to her cage.

After this incident, we knew that we would have to be keenly observant of her sexuality, and if she showed any untoward signs of affection, curtailment would have to come fast. We had always felt that nothing was wrong or unusual with this display when it occurred within the family, but we agreed that it was best not to expect others to be so accepting in the future. So we watch.

I've often thought how lucky we are that Ziggy is a mere imp and not a seventy-pound primate or larger, like a chimpanzee. The reason you never see people living with adult chimpanzees—they are always infants or pre-juveniles at best—is not only because of their strength and dangerousness, but also because of the proclivity to exercise their unbridled affections.

In *Next of Kin*, Roger Fouts talks about chimpanzee Washoe's amorous attention toward one of the male graduate students. He says, "Washoe in estrus was a force to be reckoned with. When she

developed a crush on one of my male graduate students, she would
literally throw herself at him, leaping into his arms. She would wrap
her arms around his neck, plant her wide-open mouth right over his,
and start thrusting her pelvis into his midsection."

Sexuality. Some female primates will insist on being handled by
men, and sometimes a male monkey will exhibit same-sex predilec-
tion for their human companions and will establish definitive male
pair-bonding. A monkey raised by humans is not taught about sensu-
ality, the specifics of the birds and the bees, or about copulation, yet
they exhibit a unique and individual choreography of love. Why do
some individuals suck their thumbs, while others kiss navels or smell
dirty feet? Ziggy likes chests, breasts, talking to belly buttons and
hairy armpits. She has also developed a foot fetish that takes on
strange parameters. She is filled with the *con brio* of life.

Today we are careful not to allow Ziggy to attach herself to the
head of a surprised human, stuffing her belly up against the poor
soul's face like a mask, tightly grabbing fists of hair in some kind of
primate ecstasy. We try to change the tenor of her mood, and even
change the course of the conversation—"How about those Denver
Broncos?"—and otherwise deflect the situation. I believe rejection is
not easy no matter what your species, so we handle it with kid
gloves.

In my search for all things primate-related, I have made great
friends with Ann Rademacher, a zookeeper for the great apes at the
Little Rock Zoo. And I believe, unless I operate under a braggadocio
misconception, that I have had the unique distinction of being able
to visit the chimpanzee, orangutan, and gorilla habitat separate and
apart from what the visiting public sees. In other words, I've been in
their underground homes. The great apes exhibit is set up to mimic

the animals' indigenous topography. There are cavelike depressions in the rock, a backdrop of trees and foliage, hiding places for food foraging, areas to climb, and a natural, outdoor exhibition. Inside are great caverns with smooth concrete walls (for ease in washing); large chambers, some strung with woven firehose hammocks (for hanging out and sleeping); and iron gates to separate the different species.

The day I visited was quite typical. One of the chimps filled its mouth to near overflowing and spit water at me; baby Mahale, an infant chimp, let me stroke her fingers, and the pièce de résistance, Brutus, a 450-pound silverback gorilla, made eyes at me.

At first I thought what Brutus did was an aberration. When released, he struck the big iron doors outside to display his strength and manliness. When the caretakers pushed pumpkins over the walls into his habitat, he threw a piece of pumpkin shell at my arm. Then, later, when I positioned myself up on the observation deck to get some photos, he followed my movements and *deliberately* threw a stick and, with good aim, hit my arm again! Gaining the admiration of a great gorilla is such a thrill, I cannot explain. These creatures are so awesome, really gentle giants, and his eyes, well, I can tell you that he knows precisely how to flirt. Excitedly, I told Ann about my paramour, wondering if perhaps I might be projecting my feelings onto this beast . . . was he really attracted to me? Ann looked into my eyes, gave me a wry, crooked smile, and said, "Brutus is a ladies' man."

That following Christmas I received a beautiful photo of Brutus, which I have framed and displayed in a collection with my important pictures. It serves as a memory of the day that Brutus took great pains to catch my eye.

THE MONKEY GOD

Throughout history, monkeys have been thought of in myriad ways. In India, there is the story of Hanuman, the monkey-god of Hindu mythology. Hanuman was the son of the wind god, Vayu, and a nymph. As a child he was a human, but he was swift of foot and rather reckless. One day Hanuman became enamored of the sun. Thinking it a beautiful toy, he leapt to catch it. The rambunctious child was unable to capture the sun, but his attempts upset Indra, the sky god, who sent out a thunderbolt that broke Hanuman's jaw, making his face appear apelike. Vayu, the boy's father, was enraged and wanted to destroy the heaven and earth but was dissuaded by Indra, who agreed to grant his son invulnerability.

An e-mail friend of mine, Vijay P. Mani, wrote to tell me that Hanuman was at times a naughty child and is said to have playfully troubled the saints while they were performing their rituals. Because of this annoying behavior, Hanuman incurred a curse: to forget his strengths. Consequently, he never really knows if he is strong enough to perform a particular task, and that explains why monkeys are so humble.

Hanuman figures heavily into the story of Ramayan. He saved Rama, the hero's wife, from kidnapping. For this reason, Hindus regard Hanuman as a protector. And today, millions of Indians revere monkeys as heroes of Hindu folklore. In New Delhi, monkeys are given free reign. Light brown rhesus monkeys scamper about unfettered and park themselves on fabled monuments. They also become marauding pirates, and residents must contend with their invasions into homes, markets, and I'm told, even in hospital corridors. Their mischief has reached the highest of offices; they have been found prowling the grounds of the sandstone presidential complex, on the parliament, and in the top ministerial offices they have been known to vanquish files. Iqbal Malik, a primatologist, has been asked to catch truant monkeys and relocate them to the jungle. In an Associated Press article, she said, "The problem would not have started if they had not fed the monkeys in the first place. Once the creatures get used to it, they begin demanding food. And if people don't feed them, they get hostile." Malik says that half of India's 500,000 monkeys now live in urban areas because the forests are shrinking.

India is not alone in treating monkeys and apes as sacred. In Ancient Egyptian lore, a dog-headed ape assisted Thoth and sat on the scales, weighing the heart of the deceased in the great judgment hall on the way to the afterlife. So worshipped were the apes that upon their death the ancient Egyptians embalmed them as they did all holy people and sacred cats.

China also paid homage to the monkey for centuries. The monkey is a key figure in the Chinese calendar. In the sixteenth century, stories sprang up around the adventures of a seventh-century Buddhist monk who traveled from China to India and back. In one such story, a monkey journeyed to the land of the dead and while there destroyed the forecasts of when monkeys were supposed to die, which, according to the legend, is the reason why monkeys live so long today.

A different outlook comes from the ancient Hebrews. According to the Talmud, if one sees a monkey it is a sign of bad luck. Jewish legend also has it that three classes of men built the tower of Babel, and one of those peoples was turned into apes as punishment. Some Moslems still believe that Allah turned certain ancient Jews into monkeys as punishment for having fished from the Red Sea on the Sabbath.

Sadly, modern society as a whole does not idolize monkeys or even treat them with much respect. In today's world, monkeys are netted, bludgeoned, eaten, used as bait for larger catch, experimented on, sold as pets in the underground market (most die in shipment), and generally maligned.

HELLO DOLLY

The most desired objects among Ziggy's stuffed animal coterie, the first picked to go traveling, are really toy *bears* of the teddy variety. The only other object d'amour that even remotely gets the same kind of respect is a vinyl squeaky dog toy in the shape of a yellow pear—yes, a pear—a fairly ghastly looking number with a red hat. These love-toys are fed, hauled everywhere, hugged, spoken to, peed on, slept on, and used for masturbating and grooming, sometimes to the point of their baldness. And after many years of service, their stuffing may be pulled out as in a weird, secretive, dolly liposuction, and they become, literally, a shell of their former selves.

One characteristic all these objects share is the scratched-out eyes. Ziggy performs this procedure on all her new acquisitions, apparently to ensure that they will never again have that transfixed stare that must so annoy her. After they have undergone this ritualistic disfiguring, sometimes they go through a second initiation, like a type of informal hazing, where the new object becomes "the object of disrepute." She will line them up according to the pecking order in her own head and they are the new "bad one," the one who needs a shaking up, or maybe just a few bashes against the back of the cage for thinking out loud. I've seen her cover their faces with a cloth and then jump on them, or, she will set them up in a sitting position and practice her punches (reminiscent of the old Minnie days), and if they protest, she will give them a tongue lashing, which is the vaguely the same as her "heh-heh" attack mode face. I guess you could call it her bully routine.

Soon after this series of altercations take place, a most interesting and predictable habit follows: reconciliation. Reconciliation—or peacemaking—is one of the most important characteristics capuchins use in their relationships, whether it is between dolls or individuals. Even within a wild family, you will see a mother bite her infant when it presumes too much liberty. Almost immediately after her bite, the mother will grab her infant and draw it close to her in a hug. It is similar to how many dogs unmistakably demonstrate guilt—tail between the legs, slunk-down head—when they've been caught stealing food.

Monkey reconciliation is predicated most often by a show of aggression. In studies with a variety of species, reconciliation varies from the nervous encounters of rhesus monkeys to the highly sexually charged encounters of the bonobos. With Ziggy it is the lip-smacking chatter of friendliness aimed at the offending object, person, or limb. This ritual of rapprochement must be awfully important, because if you do not allot enough time for the reconciliation to take place, she will whine and titter and make herself direly distressed. You will not get any peace until you pass reconciliation; those are her rules.

Because monkeys in the wild cannot pack their bags when someone acts aggressively toward them—the troop is vital for camaraderie and survival—they have developed mechanisms for living close, and reconciliation is one of the more powerful inclinations. Its frequency is relative to the temperament of the species; the more displays of anger, the more grooming, sublimation, or face-making that tends to take place. Using this model, some child care experts are beginning to think that children should be left alone to resolve their own disputes. Perhaps our urge to "make nice" does not allow children enough time to work it out alone, an important skill for all maturing primates.

pint-sized
and powerful

The difference between involvement and commitment?
Think ham and eggs. The chicken was involved,
the pig was committed.

RITA MAE BROWN

"Today Ziggy did another first. From the floor she crawled up the back of my legs, up past my underpants, across my back, and tried to come out the arm of my nightie. She did this twice, and the second time she got badly twisted in the armhole, but it was fun for both of us anyway." This entry in my journal is dated March 1990. Ziggy was just two months shy of her second birthday. She was growing quickly, her body strengthening with each new feat of mobility, her manipulations changing with each new desire. The mindset and skills required to "control her," were not yet part of my reality. We were

coming upon one of those times you look back on in retrospect and
say, "I wish I would have known."

We experimented by providing her with new situations and
stimulations. One time we took her on an afternoon paddleboat ride
on one of the lakes in our community. The boys were on one craft;
Ziggy was hanging out on the stern with Michael and me on
another, Michael peddling madly away. She took to the boat like an
old salt. How strange to see a monkey on the water!

Apparently, we were not the first to have a seafaring friend on
board. Hundreds of historical maritime accounts tell of monkeys and
their mischief as passengers of lading aboard cargo ships. In one particular story from the mid-nineteenth century, a merchant sailor talks
about his camaraderie with Jack, "a Cercopithecus monkey from
Senegal" (could have been a green Vervet or one of twenty-six other
subtypes). The sailor recounts that Jack was ". . . jealous of all those
of his brethren who came in contact with me, and freed himself
from two of his rivals by throwing them into the sea." Jack enticed a
small lion monkey of great beauty and gentleness to come forward,
coaxing until ". . . as he was within reach, the perfidious creature
seized him by the nape of his neck, and, as quick as thought, popped
him over the side of the ship. We were going at a brisk rate, and
although a rope was thrown out to him, the poor little screaming
thing was soon left behind, very much to my distress, for his almost
human agony of countenance was painful to behold." It was not
uncommon in the nineteenth century to see exotic monkeys on the
deck and even in the rigging of such great ships. Merchants and
sailors often took on such "live" cargo for both companionship and
the pet trade.

Surprisingly, Ziggy's love of water did not carry over to the bathtub. I guess being surrounded by five feet of cold porcelain did not suit her sensibilities. We tried sharing a bath with her—first the boys, then us—and although we were not alarmed by her eating soap, we did object to her tendency to defecate in the water if anything untoward seemed to happen—a loud noise, an unfamiliar toy. We soon found it was easier to bathe her in the kitchen sink. The space is more accommodating, and I have the spray handle to shower her clean of soap. She'll bow her head under the gentle shower and let the water cascade down over her face. Although Ziggy appears scrawny and weak when she is wet, it is a complete misrepresentation. She is pint-sized and powerful.

Monkeys possess great agility and strength. Their musculature is especially pronounced in their thighs and it winnows down to their disproportionately sized feet. They are a most beautiful representation of a finely tuned motor, so physical, so aware of their capabilities. Having a monkey is like having your own personal Olympics, every day of the year.

Even their tail is astounding, and sometimes it's my favorite part, if I can presume to divide her up into sections and parts. Although it seems to have a mind of its own, the tail is uniquely wired into the life and soul of the monkey. There are vertebrae that can be felt right down to its tip, enabling it to bend and curl at any point on the rack of bones. And the strength within it is so great that being struck by the tail unintentionally can be a lot like taking a hit from a broomstick.

Tail often acts independently of monkey, wending its way around your neck, arm, or waist as you hold its owner, and capable of surreptitious rear and flank attacks against monkey's head. At other times Tail comes to the rescue, providing backing, balance, and rigour while in the throes of the love dance, helping Ziggy clasp onto sweetheart objects and hold them close to her breast in anticipation of a pretend, but robust, copulation.

So, let's see, what do we have in this package? Enhanced eyesight; big brain; incredible strength; essentially five limbs to push, pull, and hold with; a tail that can equalize, strike, and encircle; large feet to hang on with; a tremendous will; and lightning speed. With teeth, this can be a dangerous animal.

F ALLING   O UT   OF   H ARMONY

Caps have thirty-two teeth just like humans, in the same basic configuration. They have pointed cuspids on each side, a bit more pronounced than our own, to facilitate the shred and tear with masticating. When I got bit, I couldn't believe the damage to my hands. I received three stitches in the area just under my thumb, and my hand was wrapped for a couple of days. For me, Ziggy's bite brought with it a whirlpool of emotions. The time was Thanksgiving 1991, which made Ziggy about two-and-a-half years old, in the throes of her biting period.

The bite may have been inevitable, but it was probably avoidable. I didn't observe the signpost of behavior, which was clearly indicated—if only I'd known what to look for. I didn't know enough about the intricacies of control and how to deal with friction. For an example, we can look to the dog. Dogs send very clear signals. If one dog approaches another's dish, the alpha will growl over his territorial bowl. If the approaching dog does not heed the message, most likely a fight will ensue. Straight, direct, simple. With wolves, the leader carries his head high and proud, while the others slink around below him and in greeting will gently lick the sides of his mouth in submission. Some monkeys want to ally themselves with the most powerful person, and woe to the monkey or human who holds them back. It is these subtle signals that one should learn when working with animals. Each species has its own choreography of needs, sociability, and conflict.

The situation that predicated my getting bitten was easy to recognize if I had just had the edge. I knew that Ziggy's preferences had changed. She had given plenty of signs that said, "The hierarchy has changed, lady, and you're not it, not anymore." No top dog, no big enchilada, no king of the mountain for me. Mike had become the main man, the Number One. I just didn't want to accept it or learn how to deal with it. So when Ziggy wanted to get off my lap and go to her daddy, I just held onto her tail in a kind of denial. She, in turn, reached back and changed my mind. And it was so fast, I can't say that I saw the look that said "Don't make me do this." (Yes, she has a face for that meaning.) I just didn't know what was coming. This wasn't a thinking situation; it was an emotional situation.

At the risk of sounding stereotypical, for most women, domination does not come easily. We are reared for a role of nurturing, not necessarily dominating. I remember that while raising my boys there were some days I was tired of telling them what to do and what not to do. There came a point at which it was frustrating to act as cop, counselor, teacher, nutritionist, hygienist, mediator, and control freak all rolled into one. I just wanted to throw in the towel and say, "Handle it yourselves." Most women would rather coax, instruct, and guide our children into good behavior. We would like to be able to tell them what is right and have it stick.

With some monkeys we have to assert ourselves early on and live in an almost continual alert stage. If we let down our guard, monkeys of this nature will seize the opportunity to advance. It could even be something as simple as their horning in on our preoccupied mind. When our egos get bound up in this we think, *I'm not good at training,* or, if we feel our sacrifice has been wasted and we are a failure, then all becomes extremely mired down in one big muddy relationship.

I had given Ziggy so much credit for her intelligence that I had told myself that she wouldn't bite her mother but would simply protest in a harmless way. So, when I actually got hurt, I was in a state of shock. Michael assumed all my duties with her and I laid low and worried myself into a tangle of hurt and insecurity.

Despite what I had always told visitors to our house whom Ziggy shunned—"It's not you"—I looked at her assault on me in a personal way. I told myself, "She doesn't love me or else she wouldn't have hurt me like that." That's when I called Helpings Hands. It was a call I made reluctantly. I felt a deep sense of defeat, and I didn't care to expose my pain to anyone. I had always been confident about Ziggy's love for me, and now I had to admit that I didn't know how she perceived me after all.

They were so kind. They have a way of instructing while making you think the resolution is all your idea. They also have a knack for delivering hard truths. And these are just a few of the reasons why this organization is so successful at training monkeys and handling people—two very similar acts. I was clearly beside myself, but with their guidance I was made to understand that Ziggy had already gotten her second set of teeth, and the irritability that goes along with that teething had taken on new parameters. We talked about removing her front teeth to relieve her pain and irritability sooner rather than later, because monkeys in the program will eventually have their front teeth removed anyway. They suggested we make arrangements to have Ziggy fly to Boston. That was another blow—to think that I would be the cause of her losing her teeth! My husband is fond of saying to the boys when they worry about things completely out of their control, "Deal with it." That is what I had to do and I can't say that it came easy. It was a terrible time for me.

Helping Hands was swift about making plans for Ziggy's first airplane ride. When the monkeys need to be transported, Helping Hands has arranged with certain airlines to have the employees escort the monkey, first class, back to the training center. Their support is an invaluable piece in the puzzle of monkey care.

Ziggy was absent two weeks. That was enough time to work on my personal transformation. The director called me on the phone to talk, just before Ziggy was to return home. "You can do this," she said. Then she explained how monkeys view the world, with respect to whom they will willingly follow. She told me that Ziggy still loved me, but she needed to be dealt with in a more mindful manner. And if I was to continue (and I wanted to), I would have to take into consideration how I would need to relate to my monkey during this phase.

She also told me that Ziggy had developed a kind of funny relationship with another monkey; his name was Elvis. She assured me that Ziggy "played well with others," while still maintaining her own interests, and that she had "told on Elvis" when she thought he was doing something wrong. That was exactly what I needed to hear. Laughing at Ziggy's tattling pulled me back from the brink of insecurity so that I could move onto the next level.

When Ziggy came home, I was apprehensive to say the least. The fact that she had bitten me and gotten away with it might mean she would try it again. She still had her rear molars and a chomp with her jaws would pinch, but although it might be uncomfortable, it would no longer break the skin. I felt like I was wearing a mask of confidence, hiding what was, in essence, a broken heart. I needed to get past this. It was one of the most difficult things I've ever had to do in my life. I've faced many life-altering and potentially life-threatening situations with my health, but none were quite as emotional as this.

Amazingly, all my worries seemed to quickly disappear when I realized that this experience, although traumatic for me, didn't seem to phase Ziggy at all. She ate the same food, laughed the same laugh, kissed the same kiss, and was my darling girl. The only impact removing her front teeth had was in letting me respond to her behavior instead of her teeth.

I spent a lot of time convincing myself that I could do this, with Helping Hand's guidance. One of the things they helped me to realize was that in my daily tasks with Ziggy I was forgetting to talk to her. Many of us forget this little courtesy when dealing with children. We get tired of repeating ourselves—why does a four-year-old ask the same two hundred questions every day—but we have to learn not to expect children and animals to be mind readers. We must continue to talk, to reassure our loved ones—human and animal— that we still care for and need them.

Consequently, I tell Ziggy between fifty to 100 times a day how much I love her, what a beauty girl she is, ask her if she is happy ("uh huh," she replies), and just generally gauge my love for her in any number of verbal ways. When I get Ziggy out of the cage, I tell her exactly what I want to do and suggest that she should want to do it too.

Ziggy seemed to like the new approach. I learned to give her respect by working with her opinion and her wants, and, as a bonus,

I gained her respect in return. I learned how to grab the wheel back from Ziggy and let her know who's really driving when I needed to, by utilizing several quick ways of regaining my ground.

For example, if she attempts to bite or succeeds in biting me, I take my thumb and press down on her palate until she's ready to spit it out. It isn't a crushing pressure, but just enough to be uncomfortable. Frans de Waal tells a story about working with capuchins where he thought the ones who had befriended him—shown him the most friendly intentions—would be the easiest to train. He says that the tamest ones were actually the ones who gave him the most trouble. They started a major brawl when he wanted them to go into a carrier for a particular test. He felt he had earned their trust and now he says, he had ". . . the temerity to violate all their expectations. They screamed and barked, lunged at me, slapped at my face, but also made friendly sounds in between their bouts of rage, as if pleading with me to call off the whole business." He claims the capuchins operated on the notion that, because they felt they had developed a bond, they assumed this fact should give them some leverage. De Waal continues, "Not wanting to hurt them, but also not prepared to let them get away with their behavior, I simply showed more patience and determination than they were willing to invest. In a few cases it took an hour before the monkey finally entered the carrying case, leaving both of us exhausted. The same individuals would enter in ten minutes on the next day, then in five, until they would try to go into the transport cage even before I had opened it." Not having read that passage in 1991, I still felt in my bones that that was how it had to go: in patient, two-four time, and the beat had to be consistent.

Another thing I learned was how to apply a restraint when I sensed a situation might be leaving the gentle track. I would do one of two things: If Ziggy was standing, I would take hold of her arms and pin them in a collected clasp behind her back. Monkeys have a lot of appendages that may keep on moving—the feet can curl up in a ball, the tail will seek an object with which to push off, it's the wiggle factor—but it's surprising that when the arms are held firmly in this pin, the monkey is induced to settle down. Holding their limbs in gentle restraint sends an important signal to the rebellious brain that says, ". . . it's okay, you're still a good girl."

The other position that most closely resembles this posture is to pin her on the ground. Not the ground literally—it can be a couch, a chair, or even my lap; but the movement is this: I pick her up and lay her on her back with her shoulders pinned by her side and then look down at her and say, "Settle down." Not loud, not anxious, but with the demeanor of, "Look, you've forgotten your place; see? I am bigger and can put you on your back; you'd best remember who is the boss and I am going to do this to remind you."

Paula Puckett, foster mother to Emma, also uses the pin method. She places Emma in her lap and pins Emma while at the same time waiting for her to calm down. Paula says, "She reacts like a child. When she's done something wrong, she knows it. And sometimes she'll come up afterward to hug me to apologize." Monkeys instinctively want to please, but if they are reprimanded for something they've done wrong, some may lash out at a scapegoat, usually the person they feel they can get away with picking on. It's a way of blaming their troubles on someone else. It is not much different from a spouse who takes out his job disappointments on his most loving companion, his wife, or a child who blames his sibling for something he did to avoid getting in trouble. We primates have a tendency to take advantage of our loved ones, knowing that we can get away with venting because they will always be there for us. Of course, this redirection of aggression can go too far.

Today the much older Ziggy will sometimes disassociate my feet as belonging to my body if I'm lying in a recliner. If I reprimand her, she wants to put blame on the nearest underling around (the pecking order of hierarchy in full swing), and my feet take the lowest position on the totem pole. So they get picked on. It's just her head trip. The current rule is feet are separate, they do not belong to me, so they are the target of disrepute. If I can figure out a way to distract her enough or use another calming technique, maybe she will give it up. I'm still working on it, to tell you the truth.

Other times, when we're in the recliner, Ziggy makes peeping "love noises" over my feet, so maybe it is a love/hate relationship after all. She will take off my shoes and smell the inside. Next comes the sock stripping. She inserts her entire arm down the length of my sock to the sole, and then turns it inside-out until it comes off. Next she will mouth my toes. I have to do everything I can to keep from laughing because my feet are very sensitive and I wouldn't want to deter her from the ritual. Next she places soft, whiskerlike kisses on my toes and grooms them carefully with her fingers, picking between each digit, removing stray sock stuff in a very earnest manner. This is a profound, predictable pattern and always follows these same precise small steps. Such a ritual, but it seems to please. It makes me smile. Who am I to deny?

I wish I'd had the edge from the beginning. The edge is control. Nothing more than parental control. It is about being clear and consistent, about working with Ziggy or any child with conviction of purpose. It does not come easily to a lot of humans, least of all me. Sometimes, as an adolescent, Ziggy was a hyper little rascal on a leash, bouncing off walls and flailing around, a boinging Betty. I should have started then. I had to learn to deal with conflict in more direct, judicious ways—not by being fierce or punitive—but by giving more physical body language, and giving it in more definite ways than some of us are used to. I could have saved myself a lot of heartache and wasted emotions had I paid attention. I could have turned to Helping Hands earlier and gotten some sage advice. The saving grace is that perhaps these stories will serve as insight into monkey care, and others can skip over my mistakes and build on their own.

From time to time, Ziggy still persists in getting the best of me! It reminds me of those hilarious old Peter Sellers "Pink Panther" movies. Inspector Clouseau wants to maintain his superiority of adroitness and dexterity in order to deal with the crooks; therefore, he has Cato, his faithful aide, attack him at the most unseemly times to keep him on his toes. So we see this bumbling inspector trying to look official, make love, or attend to the report, and Cato is there behind the door, springing on poor old Clouseau at the most inopportune moments. Well, guess what? Ziggy is my Cato.

LIONS AND TIGER AND BEARS, OH MY

If you don't have a clear idea of how you come off to others, spend time with a monkey. They have a tendency to act the little barometer. If the family falls into a fight, the monkey gets upset: bristling hair, teeth-baring grin, lots of charging, and sometimes throwing objects onto the floor. If one family member chastises another, monkeys are great at pointing the finger.

One time I was walking past Ziggy's cage carrying a large box. Monkeys tend to fear the unknown, and something about that box apparently freaked her out. She rattled the cage bars. The noise scared me because I was operating in Never Never Land. Angered, I started making noise in her direction, *in toto* with some of the decibels she had used on me. Michael observed this scene and said that our actions mirrored each other. And so it goes. We've become so attached that at times we reflect each other's moods and actions. Anger begets anger, silly begets silly, and dopey is more than a dwarf.

Monkeys are fearful of the damnedest things. I fully understand how strange and scary it must be for her when birds or bats get trapped in our house. Every year we have a bird's nest in the garage and more often than once misdirected birds have flown into the house. A bird flapping in and out of three levels, up into the skylight and past the french doors is one frantic bird, and Ziggy will make laps around the cage, pointing and "heh-hehhing" all over the place. Understandable—it is not like us. The bat was scary, too. It had apparently hung out in the house all day and did not make itself known until we turned out the lights to watch a late-night movie. Then its sonar kicked into gear and it was practically impossible to catch. Ziggy shrieked and ran and ran around and around, trying to tell us to "catch that thing." You'd have thought it was the devil.

One Halloween the boys scared the willies out of Zig. Their masks—one a bulldog and the other a werewolf—were those full-face, soft, rubbery ones, so no matter that the body underneath smelled and looked like Jordan, or that the jeans and shoes were definitely Courtney's, to Ziggy it was still a monster. She inched her way backward into the corner of the cage—and left behind feces, bringing new meaning to the term *scared shitless.* Then she covered her head with a cloth.

There are other things that scare Ziggy too. Our boys grew up with a three-foot doll dressed like a farmer; it has big ruddy cheeks and a cigar in its mouth that simply drives Ziggy batty. She will carry on an entire seige with that yokel doll; backing up, charging, displaying her ferociousness, and backing off again. It's never moved, so apparently the danger is all in her head.

Other stuffed animals play the nemesis, too, and sometimes I like to line them up on the bed. I got the idea when Zig spotted a stuffed baboon and her child in a basket on the floor. One day, I couldn't figure out what she was complaining about until I looked over the edge and saw the offending object. How dare those primates reside under there! Well, I've added a gorilla, an orangutan, and a small spider monkey, all of which play the rival now. She knocks them over and just generally vents. We play like this on a semi-regular basis. Those big bad animals just seem to ask for it.

individual or instinct?

God has given you one face, and you make yourself another.

WILLIAM SHAKESPEARE

Living with a primate is always an adventure. Even during the slower, dull-average days where time is marked by meals there is always something interesting to observe. Just before I wrote this paragraph, I played with Ziggy. I swung her up on my calf, holding her hands tightly and lifting her up and down in the air like a child riding a hobby horse. Then I stopped her from knocking over the garbage, blew on a kazoo to amuse her, and changed her diaper. Later, I learned a little more about the mix between mischief and cooperation when I let her climb into my shirt while trying to keep her from typing.

This chapter is therefore a shared effort, made possible by my knowledge of her. Knowing her and her capabilities and understanding how she sees things is ultimately the most important facet of primate care. The greater a monkey's intelligence, the greater the capacity for unexpected or curious and creative behavior.

I've often wondered what habits, what little traits of behavior were unique to Ziggy. Which tendencies were individual or instinctual? Like any life form, monkeys have singular valleys of conduct that resist the normal mapping. A few behaviors that I thought were peculiar to Ziggy turned out to be not so unusual after all.

TICKLE

I had read many reports from Jane Goodall, Roger Fouts, and others about chimpanzees who were ticklish or wanted to engage in games of "tickle me." Of course, juvenile great apes desire contact, and tickle games with their elders provide lots of that. Tickling can be both a tool for reward and a kind of bribery for desired behaviors. (I have never come across any literature about *monkeys* and tickling.)

Although I've seen young monkeys respond with a kind of ecstatic gaiety—foster mother Paula Puckett can make her Emma join in on a session of excited glee just by screeching—I've never found Ziggy to be ticklish. It's more fun for her if you contain her head in your hands like a modified wrestling hold where she will roll into a ball and initiate mouthing and play. We often blow raspberries on her feet and although that would drive me crazy, she remains aloof. Maybe the soles of her feet are toughened up from all the climbing and prehensile activity required of them.

Body Chatter

I used to think that talking to belly buttons or armpits and sucking on earlobes were conformities unique to Zig. Such a funny little oddity, the belly button fetish. I soon learned by talking to others that some monkeys love certain body parts, like feet and belly buttons. And they are generally so thrilled with encountering a hairy armpit that they will spring into lip-smacking chatter.

"So what's your monkey doing now?"

"Oh, she's talking to my belly button!"

Along with the favor bestowed on belly buttons and armpits, Zig will lick my face in greeting and sometimes stick a long quick tongue up each nostril as part of her salutation protocol. Everyone in the family has gone through this initiation. Jordan described it well, saying it felt like her darting tongue went "clear up to my brain!" This must be an instinct compatible with grooming, and again, I found out it is not unique to our own little monkey girl. (By the way, it's not as icky as it sounds; just a natural, normal part of a monkey's system of personal hygiene.)

Wearing Clothes—or Not!

Wearing clothes is a struggle for our monk. Like a preteen in her first bra, the straps and other accoutrements just don't suit her sensibilities. She will let you push an infant's tee shirt and soft sweater over her head, but once tethered to the tree outside, she will promptly pull it off. I used to be jealous of the other monkeys pictured in the Helping Hands newsletter wearing tiny sweatsuits, dresses, and jackets. But monkeys are all different. One particular little guy liked wearing a sock or headband around his chest, another likes long white gloves, and still many others sleep with fluffy sweatshirts. I suppose if you orient them to clothing early on, they will wear little Oshkosh overalls or Baby Gap apparel with ease. But I do not have a clotheshorse in Ziggy.

I recently saw a documentary called *The Snow Monkeys of Texas* by director/producer Richard M. Lewis. Hot Springs has a Documentary Film Festival of world-renown proportions and my husband and I made a point of catching this twenty-three-minute short and the question-and-answer session that followed. *The Snow Monkeys of Texas* is the charming tale of how 150 Japanese snow macaques were moved from their environment in the cold snowy regions of Japan's mountains to the arid brush and desert surroundings of south Texas. These monkeys had braved snowstorms and were acclimated to the treacherous environment in the mountains of Japan. They subsisted on tree bark through harsh winters when leaves and shrubs were scarce.

The documentary tells of their initial hardships in Dilley, Texas— of learning respect for rattlers, cactus, and cowboys—and how the troop, without predators, grew into an unruly and dangerous group of more than five hundred, and then how the balance of troop life was met finally one more time. It is a story of hope, a terrible clash with humans, and the triumph of the primate spirit.

The thick, furry coat of the Japanese macaques thinned as the animals adapted to the sweltering heat of the arid Texas region. The pads on their buttocks that kept them from freezing their extremities in the highlands helped to protect their seats in the bristling heat of the Texas sun. And the same spirit and will to live that allowed them to survive in the cold mountains of Japan helped them to thrive in the dry, desertlike regions of south Texas. Here in Arkansas we do get all four seasons, though the winter is pretty mild. Ziggy's coat gets long and silky in October, as her body adapts to the changes in the climate, just like those snow monkeys in the documentary.

TELEPHONE PROBLEMS

Still looking for behaviors singular to Zig, I thought perhaps one unique characteristic might be her animosity toward the telephone. I don't enjoy phone conversations myself, and I wondered if it might be something I'd transmitted to her through my own behavior. Doreen, our foster parent advisor, has trained her monkey to be tolerant of the telephone because she is on it virtually every day, all day, answering questions and following up with foster families. Emily, Doreen's foster monkey and ward, doesn't try to cut up as much when Doreen "chats" anymore because she has realized that it's part of the drill with living with her mom.

I read a story in the late 1980s about a monkey baby, Jessica, and her surprised foster mother, who seemed obviously new to the program. Jessica's foster parent wrote that one day Jessica was out of the cage when the telephone rang. The mother answered the call in the kitchen and was engaged in conversation when she heard the extension being picked up in the other room. Apparently Jessica heard her mother talking on the line, so she started yapping into the receiver, too. The mom then asked Jessica over the phone if she was hungry. The monkey dropped the receiver and ran to the kitchen, dashed across the counter, and brought her mother her dish and spoon! Conversation was apparently not lost on that telephone-eavesdropping monkey.

Ziggy dislikes telephones and telephone talking a lot. If I'm holding her and the phone rings and I answer it, she will try to push the buttons, bite the receiver, and generally try to disrupt me. I have gotten her to squeak or "talk" to others over the phone, but she'd just as soon skip the whole matter. Are there telemarketers out there who are monkey owners? I can't imagine the odds of those two ever coming together are very good.

E A T I N G   G E L   I N   T H E   D I A P E R S

We only put a diaper on Ziggy when we know she will be out of her cage for longer than half an hour. A few times we've forgotten to take the diaper off before she reenters the cage. When this happens, she immediately pulls the diaper down over her hips. Then she proceeds to make a toy of it: pulling off the tabs, poking at Barney on the plastic logo part, and shredding it to a pulpy mess. One day, I saw her *eat* some of the soft padding. I quickly took the mess away, to her dismay, and made a mental note to ask Doreen when she called next, "What the hell was that all about?" I had thought that this little peculiarity, diaper grazing, would finally be a behavior completely unique to Zig, a solitary oddity only my quirky Ziggy would be capable of devising in order to drive me crazy. No such luck. It turns out that diaper manufacturers put "gel"—like gelatin—in the padding to help soak up liquids. The strange chemistry of the liquid on the padding is what attracted Ziggy. If you ever see a monkey eating a diaper, you will know they are either extremely bored or in need of a helping of Jell-O.

Hygiene isn't much of an issue in the wild. In a primate's arboreal habitat, their refuse and feces naturally fall to the ground out of the trees. The jungle floor is rich with nutrients and quick to compost. As the group is always on the move, there is little risk of an area becoming fouled or smelly. Even the great apes that bed down in nests and defecate within those chambers make a new sleeping quarter at a new site each night.

It's a different matter entirely with hand-reared primates. Monkeys at Helping Hands are taught to pee and defecate in their cage before they come out, to keep the area clean and sanitary. I've read commentaries from monkey owners on the Internet, though, stories about monkeys peeing into electronics and just generally making bad mistakes. With proper attention and, above all, consistency, monkeys can be taught to eliminate appropriately, expanding their social purview, making them popular guests.

ladder of emotions

*God gave us our memories
so that we might have roses in December.*
JAMES MATTHEW BARRIE

We turn to animals when we're perplexed with the world, asking them for loyalty, comfort, and understanding. We even use them and their behavior in comparative analysis to keep our egos inflated. We want to be able to measure ourselves and our idiosyncrasies against those of a presumed "lesser, intellectual world" [not my words]. Scientists attach electrodes to the heads of little critters, looking for answers to all sorts of questions about human behavior.

Few of us with pets can say that we do *not* project our own feelings onto our animals. Through our own conceits and inventions, we presume to talk for them. We put words into their mouths as if they were commenting on the state of a meal, the frigid temperature outside, or what they think of the mutt next door. Why else would dogs suffer Sherpa fleece coats and Goretex hats and the little human accoutrements of winter?

We project what we're thinking on animals and we anthropomorphize (attribute human emotions onto their character), coloring our view of the animal's experience as only we can. Learned primatologist Frans de Waal claims he tries to look at the behavior of animals from the animals' viewpoint, taking into account their feelings, expectations, and intelligence. He says, "Provided that it is based on intimate knowledge and translated into testable hypotheses, anthropomorphism is a very useful first step toward understanding a psychology similar to and almost as complex as ours."

I project onto Ziggy almost every day. If forced, the rest of my family would admit that they do it too. When I am eating something that Ziggy should not have, I offer her a suitable substitute, believing that her feelings will be hurt if I do not. Food as reward, food as sustenance, food as comfort—our human preoccupation with food results in overfed animals and monkeys with poor health.

When I am out shopping and the day turns into a series of parking rifts and long lines, I worry that Ziggy will be "mad" at me for being gone so long. My husband has said it numerous times also; and he uses this unconscious transfer of feelings as a convenient reason to depart from an overly long social event or indulgent shopping blowout. "We've got to go," he'll say. "Your little girl will be angry that you've left her home alone." Indeed, in some instances, this has been borne out.

Last summer I took an important course in forensic facial reconstruction sculpture, a significant discipline in another area of my life and expertise, forensics. The class was held at the Cleveland Institute of Art, and, although it meant a plane trip, I would be able to see other family members and save costs by staying with my in-laws, so I could not find a reason not to go. My son acted as sitter for Ziggy. When I returned after a week's absence, Ziggy and I had a terrible row. It happened while I was giving her a bath in the kitchen sink. She decided it was a good time for retribution, administered a chomp on my hand, and tried to exit my control, soaking wet. Michael and Jordan were goofing around on the steps nearby, but they grew instinctively quiet and nonintrusive, knowing that this would be a gap Ziggy and I would have to bridge one-on-one. I was baffled, imagining what Zig was thinking. Hadn't I given her baths without incident for more than nine years? What other conditions could have led to this cruelty on her part other than her anger over my long absence? How could I depersonalize it?

Sometimes I will put her back in the cage and feel unkind and punitive, worrying that she will love me a little less. This is *my* hang-up. In actuality, she is probably more than willing to return to her "apartment"—to eat her own snacks, talk to her animals privately, or turn the keys on a toy. She needs her own defined space as well as we do when the pressures around us grow dense.

I try to excuse my "scriptwriting-her-life" tendencies because Ziggy can feel like many people to me—best friend, child, older protective brother, lover—that's why I feel uniquely qualified to assess what she may know or experience. And who, dear Reader, thinks that animals have no soul? I personally believe it's better to err on the side *for* soul. Unfortunately, there are too many people in the world who act as if animals are nonentities. In another one of my studies, criminal profiling—matching personality impulses to a crime—I have learned that the incidence of animal mutilation and cruelty in childhood is a recurrent characteristic of adult sadistic murderers and psychopaths. These corrupt personalities have no compunctions about quashing another being's feelings and their dispassionate behavior occurs early on and with perverse regularity.

JEALOUSY

"You love that monkey more than you love me."

Although no one in my family has ever said those words, there are times when my steadfast rituals with Ziggy may have seemed like a slight to the others who were engaged in more family related goings-on at the time. Good thing my life partners have an independent streak. Prospective foster families should be aware: Monkeys can divide a family by the different relationships they impose on each member—whether by liking one best above all others or by using their scapegoating to pick on their least favorite person, usually the youngest or least attentive family member.

Sometimes they will insist on being handled by certain people only in private, or they will settle down when there is one person in the room at a time. For some monkeys, it seems as if the addition of another personality is too much for them to take—like Jack, the monkey who threw other species overboard from the deck of a great sailing ship when he determined they might command too much attention from his "mate"—as if the others were taking something away from him.

My poor mother has suffered countless aggressions from our monkey. Ziggy is extremely jealous of her, knowing that my attention will be diverted when Mom is around. She insists on acting the beast, cage-rattling, and displaying. She has played "Bonzai!" on my mother's head, cried loudly over her talking, and jumped up her arm to bite her. My mother, Anna, grew up on a farm and instinctively freezes when something like this happens. She knows that a fixed posture with hands held to the side can be a deterrent against a charging dog or another animal that displays aggression. Ziggy's actions toward Anna are more disruptive than dangerous, but it is disconcerting for me to see such evidence of jealousy.

One thing to note is that Ziggy will immediately begin lip-smacking after her transgression. She makes a rapid emotional shift from anger to friendliness. This is an important attempt at reconciliation. Monkeys seem to have an inherent sense that tells them it is best to "make up" and do it quickly, sometimes in the same breath. No sooner has she done the deed than the lips start to quiver. It's as if she's telling my mother, "The green-eyed monster made me do it. Look at me. See how cute I am. Get over it. I couldn't help myself." Anna reassures Ziggy by telling her everything's all right. If my mother were asked to explain it, I'm sure she would say it's one of those things her daughter got her into and she loves us anyway.

All of these feelings are present on the ladder of emotions. The emotions felt by others around us, the emotions we suffer silently, and the emotions we project onto others. And who can say what the emotions of another really are? Human or not. That's why the studies with chimps learning American Sign Language have proved so psychologically enlightening. One story has it that when Roger Fouts got a poke from a chimp named Loulis, Roger made a big deal of it, crying and acting out. Later, Fouts says, whenever he showed Loulis the scratch to make him feel guilty, Loulis would squeeze his eyes tight and refuse to look. He didn't want to talk about his attack or even look at the scratch. Could we say this was remorse? If not, I don't know what is. But basically, we're projecting again.

The Party's Not Here

Ziggy sometimes shows her worst side when new people are thrown into the mix. She has kept us from entertaining friends at home. Sure, we've had hundreds of people pass through our lives and our house over the years, including foreign exchange students and an immoderate number of teenage boys spending the weekend. But when it comes to providing dinner for another couple, or enjoying a quiet evening of conversation, we prefer to go out. Our best friends understand and make allowances, acting as our perpetual hosts.

When toddlers are introduced to strangers, they will often hide behind their mother's legs and peek around, or hang off her hip in coy resistance. Ziggy will assume one of several postures. She may circle the cage in a nervous frenzy, having inflicted quick judgment on the intruder, and show us what she thinks by scratching her arms and legs in an irritated manner—the stressed stance. Or she will retreat to the back of the cage, acting scared or uncommunicative, when she knows damn well the newcomers are just approaching for a look-see and are totally nonaggressive. Otherwise, why would we have let them in the house? I call this the resistant-to-change attitude. Other times she has become disruptive. I once held a small "host family" orientation in my home for a foreign exchange family candidate, and throughout the process of my showing posters and giving instruction on a student's adaptation techniques, Ziggy was screaming, yes, screaming, to let us know that in no uncertain terms was she to be ignored. "How dare those people look at cardboard signs and papers when they could be looking at me. *Me!*"

Occasionally she will make other people feel like they are wel-come. "Yes," her behavior says, "You should come closer and pet me. . . . Come laugh at me and let me entertain you . . ." as if she were a lady of the night. Shameless.

Monkeys are not fools. They want attention and love just like any-body else. They are jealous but they are also loving. As Judi Zazula, head trainer and executive director of Helping Hands, says: "There is *nothing* in the world like being chosen by a monkey for attention."

In a change of heart and hierarchy, I have again become the main love object with the adult Ziggy, and it makes me very, very happy. Monkeys are capable of hugging—their best feature in my estimation—something you cannot get from "man's best friend," the dog. They are also comical to watch and enjoy. When monkeys are raised in a comfortable and nurturing home environment, they can deliver all the love and companionship anyone could hope for. And when they establish a relationship with a quadriplegic, it adds immeasurable joy to his or her life. I firmly believe that even if the monkeys didn't per-form any tasks at all for the disabled, they would still provide an invaluable service. They provide a unique psychological lift, a com-panion with no built-in prejudices, a loving and contented friend. Just as the Seeing Eye dog gives a blind person more autonomy, so a monkey friend provides independence for a disabled person.

GUILT

When Ziggy and I return from a walk, I've taken to attaching her leash to the bottom of a couch leg in order to clean her cage in peace. That way, she can roam a respectable area and I do not have to chase her throughout the house, wondering what she is getting in to.

Her curiosity almost always overrules her common sense and, of course, I do not want her to suffer the consequences of drinking cleaning fluid or any number of other possibilities. In her childlike exuberance, she will pick up the cellular phone and study its face, turn off the television, and pry open the lids on tins. Occasionally, she will find my husband's breath mints and begin to unwrap this booty, popping one into her mouth while taking out another. She generally has no problem with my taking away the mints; she gives them up without any protest. But when I give her "the look" that says to put something down, such as a very interesting envelope or container, you would think I was the wicked stepmother. Acting the little Sarah Bernhardt, she will clasp her hands together, tilt her head to the side, and cry the whiny wails of protest that can only be assigned the label of *guilt.* It's as though she's saying, "I know it looked bad for me, but why not? Why not? Why not?" All of this takes place before I've even uttered the words, "Put it back."

There's an amusing story in a book entitled *Man Meets Dog,* a loving account about animals written by Konrad Lorenz. This particular tale concerns the attempts of some zookeepers to outwit an orangutan. The director of the Amsterdam Zoo at that time, J. Portielje, often used a distraction technique in order to get a slow-moving, lazy, Sumatran orangutan to take his exercise. The keepers were instructed to place a little food at the very top of the cage in order to force the great beast to make the upward climb for his banana. This method had the dual benefit of making the animal "work" for the food—a variation on foraging—and facilitating the large motor exercise it so badly needed. This same technique was used by the keepers when it came time to clean the cage. While one keeper kept the ape occupied with food at the top of the cage, the other quickly cleaned the floor below with a broom and bucket. On one occasion the orangu-tan took exception to the rule and suddenly came sliding down the bars and bolted for the door. Lorenz says, "Although both Portielje and the keeper exerted all their strength in an attempt to close it, the orangutan pulled it slowly but surely back, inch by inch. When it was just open enough for the animal to escape, Portielje was struck by a bright idea, such as can only occur to a past master of animal psychology. He suddenly released the door and, jumping back with a loud cry, gazed, as though horrified, at a point immediately behind the orangutan. The animal spun around in an instant to see what was going on behind it and in the same moment the door snapped in the lock." Of course, mere seconds passed before the ape realized it had been duped and flew into a righteous rage. Lorenz claims there was no question the ape knew it had been a victim of a "premeditated falsehood."

GAZE AVERSION: AN EMOTIONAL REACTION?

A behavioral trait all monkeys and apes share is gaze aversion. Some primatologists theorize it is related to hierarchy: a monkey's cognizance of its place in relation to the troop as a whole. Frans de Waal believes that it may be one of many moves involved in a face-saving tactic. Others think averting the eyes shows deference to the older and more powerful. Zookeepers and others who work around primates will tell you that gaze aversion is the best approach with which to greet a newcomer. Others surmise gaze aversion may be the white flag of embarrassment. In fact, truth be known, it is the observers at a zoo who seem to embarrass the primate subjects on display.

Humans will "ape" what they think is animal behavior. You will see teens and adults alike, acting up, speaking with loud voices and using overly dramatic and obscene gestures where they drop and curl their arms, pretend to scratch their armpits or mimic some other overture they think fits an ape's comportment. At most zoos there are signs posted urging people to use normal speaking tones and not try to antagonize the species by acting boisterous or aggressive. What a sad lot can pass through zoo exhibits in the guise of observers. Who is acting primal? Mostly it is the humans. By nature, monkeys are a cautious but fairly quiet lot. It's not until they are faced with danger or the threat of the unknown that "all hell breaks loose."

Personally, I like to think that gaze aversion is more linked with waiting for *the honest face.* I have no scientific hypothesis to espouse and no hard data or field research from which to draw, but through my observations with Ziggy and the several other species I've watched over the years, the averted glance feels like a form of respect for the calm, the pre-possessed. It implies, "Yes, I would like to look at you, but looking is played in this particular game as a coy move. You glance, I look away—but I will watch you candidly until you catch my eyes again." It's almost as if the monkey is a photographer waiting for the spontaneity that so often escapes the rehearsed pose. The poser wants to present a look that captures his "best side" or nicest smile, but the face captured on film is but a shadow of the statement that a truly expressive face can hold. These are the faces—the unaffected visages—that monkeys maneuver to see.

COMPASSION

Binti Jua was nominated animal hero of the year in *Newsweek's* "100 Newsmakers of 1996." What she did to earn this distinction surprised a lot of people, but not me or my family. Binti is a 150-pound lowland gorilla who lives at the Brookfield Zoo in Illinois. She garnered media attention for her rescue of a three-year-old boy who fell eighteen feet into the gorilla compound. After the child fell, Binti stroked and cradled the youngster, then carried him to a door where zoo staff members were waiting to and transport him to the hospital.

I had an experience where I anticipated a reassuring, compassionate reaction from Zig and received none. Ziggy and I were having a tiff that I alone perpetuated. I should have known better than to handle her when I was upset. I was bemoaning the fact my career had stalled; I felt tortured, small, and insignificant. I was crying the deep sobs of repressed anger, and although I know she does not weather my stress well—it has a tendency to get her keyed up—for some reason I expected her to be my relief. I bent into her body to get a hug and she accidentally scratched my eye.

At first I thought my eyelashes got brushed. Then it felt irritated as though something was in my eye. Flushing it with artificial tears provided no relief, and throughout the night the symptoms became much worse. Eventually, it began to feel as if there was a stone in my eye. I had an extreme sensitivity to light and continual waves of tears washed over my field of vision. I experienced a terrible, long, and painful night until I could visit the eye doctor the next morning. What little sleep I got was spent sitting up in a lounge chair.

For three days I was blind. The doctor prescribed antibiotics, and I had to wear a patch until the corneal epithelium—the clear protective window that shields the eye—healed. The cornea is filled with many nerve endings and any scratching of the surface is very painful. (I'm told most scratched corneas typically come from playing with young children or during contact sports.) And because our eyes contain an intricate network of interconnected muscles, opening one eye caused pain in the other.

In a strange way, this hurt was a fortuitous rift in time for me. It knocked me to my senses. I am a very independent person, somewhat of a control freak about my surroundings. Being taken out of the game, albeit temporarily, while life continued as usual for everyone else made me feel very fragile and insignificant. I was lucky enough to come out of it fairly unscathed, but I was reminded how too often we forget the ones who are taken out of the forward march in any one of a hundred different ways; and how we must not forget those who are struggling to keep up.

So much of life is spent in the pursuit of self-gratification. It's a cruel awakening when you discover there are a lot of people out there who do not have the luxury of movement, sight, or hearing, and you could become one of them in a blink. This ordeal tripped some kind of switch inside me that has given me a new outlook, and I trust it will make a difference somewhere down the line.

TRUST

Trust is hard to describe. An ethereal feeling, the dictionary still defines it in concrete terms: "A firm belief in the reliability, truth or strength of a person or thing; a confident expectation . . ." In her younger days, Ziggy had what you might call "trust issues." Every time I would remove an empty, dirty dish from her feeding cup, she'd climb up on the bars at eye level, tip that little head of hers 30 degrees, and cry like a baby. Her feeding insecurity would not have earned her a placecard in purgatory, but the habit was very annoying just the same.

Why, for heaven's sake, would she think I was taking something away? Surely she knew that the removal of one cup would be followed by its replacement with a full one. If the cup switch were done with a full cup already in hand for her to see, the whiny display was much less severe, but she would still pitch a fit as if not to disappoint.

During her adolescence, we had to tell her to "Get down in the corner" to wait for her food cup because she would try to scratch the hand taking the dirty empty away. Over the years this starving man's habit has dissipated, but I think it must have been an instinctive urge and one that has been only gradually suppressed due to our consistent displays of generosity with her.

Another show of trust that has developed over time reminds me of the "trust game" in which one person falls backward from a standing position, trusting that their partner will catch them. Once, when I was teaching Jordan a dancing move—the dip—he assured me of his competence, only to let me drop to the floor! Today I do not fall for that mistake, no matter how much he assures me of his readiness. Let's say, I am *not* the Rogers to his Fred Astaire.

But Ziggy has become *my* Ginger Rogers. I noticed this occurrence just this year, as a matter of fact. I will open the cage, and if she is not quite ready, I will reach in to get her. If she happens to be sitting on the top of her "bedroom"—a wire milk crate welded onto the side of the cage over my head—she will free fall to the left and into my hand, which is held out in the air awaiting her arrival. I don't remember when we first coordinated this move, but her body is a convenient glove-sized handful, and it is one of the pleasures of my day to catch her. I just reach up with my hand and she literally falls into my grip. And of course I've never dropped her. Fred Astaire would be proud.

W H E N   T O   B E   G O O D

Once, when the day was especially difficult for me and I was feeling rather put out by the efforts of caring for two teenage boys, a husband, a dog, a monkey, and a house, I talked to my husband about sending Ziggy back to Helping Hands. I can't say for certain, but I think she may have overheard me discussing this disaffection with my husband and it prompted a shift in her behavior. She became a model monkey after that—a real pleasure to have around. Of course, I don't really know what precipitated the change, but I think we must be careful about what we say about others—even animals—that can hurt. Words are powerful and can have lasting consequences on our psyche, our conduct, and how we feel about ourselves. As far as I'm concerned, verbal abuse is virtually as damaging as physical abuse, although I do not know in reality what either is like. I remember a verse from a love poem that goes like this: "I wish I could climb inside your mouth and ride on every word you speak." It would be a fine world indeed if we could all feel and understand the weight of that sentiment.

U S E F U L   Z I G G Y

When you ask Ziggy to do something she doesn't understand, such as "Give me the metal thing," she will turn around and lift her butt up in the air. I take this as a cooperative move. She wants to please. For this reason and a hundred similar indications, I truly believe that monkeys like to work.

I once saw a documentary about a small merchant (both in stature and in industry) and his macaque, a blond, snout-nosed beauty. Macaques are strong, large, hardy stock. They are often feisty, have incredible will, and have become the mainstay of the medical research community. (I know this because I once visited a research facility and wrote a about how they used macaques in pharmaceutical tests—but that story is for another book.) This man and his monkey lived on an island replete with coconut trees. The old man taught his primate companion how to climb trees and collect coconuts.

This is extremely difficult work. The nuts are lodged at the top of swaying, fifty-foot palm trees. The vines that hold the heavy fruits are thick and unyielding, and it is strenuous, physical work getting them loose. The monkey would balance on the tree's trunk with his arms and tail, and grab the fruit between his feet and twist and twist the fleshy cording until the troublesome fruit gave way, falling to the ground below. The monkey worked up to six-hour days with just a short period of respite for lunch (which they shared). The old man loved this monkey, and after the day's toil he would lead his monk through the woods, over some rocks, and down to a running stream to an area where the water and rock landscape created a small clear pool. There he would sit and massage his monkey's feet and legs under the water, lovingly rubbing out the aches and cricks from a hard day's efforts. They made a good team.

One day, his wife struck a private deal, selling the monkey without the old man's knowledge. The old man was heartsick when he found out and made no attempt to hide his pain. His wife soon discovered that the pairing was vital for both the old man and his monkey aide. Being together was, in major part, their life's work; they created work for each other. The man had been good to his monkey, and they had even won a competition for speed-collecting coconuts that was held annually in the village. The wife realized she had to buy the monkey back, and peace was restored.

I'm not saying that all animals should be workhorses, but for some animals, the work that they do is valuable, not only to their mates, but for their own well-being. If they don't have real work, then exercise should substitute. Animals who are valued seem to know and relish their importance, as do humans. When I am in the front yard working on my garden, I tether Ziggy on a long, twenty-foot chain to a large hardwood tree, and she mimics my work. If I am digging a hole, I provide her with child-sized implements and she will dig holes. If I do not give her plastic tools, I see her collect sticks to dig holes with. In an afternoon she moves rocks, picks both flowers and weeds, traps bugs, and climbs the tree to serve as watchmaster. Of course an ample amount of time is spent simply lounging in the crook of the tree, but she also balances this with her other "chores." Just as young children like to imitate vacuuming, driving a car, and baking treats in a play oven, so monkeys like to work.

In the house it is no different. Ziggy likes to take a rag and wipe down surfaces and even scrub her walls and cage floor with wipes. Work makes people *and primates* feel real. Take away their work and you take away their worth. All you need to do to prove this hypothesis is interview the unemployed, the disabled, or the disenfranchised. Feeling useful is vital to happiness. So if you drive by and see Ziggy busily digging a hole or positioning a rock, tell her she's doing a good job, okay?

other voices

I am a man of fixed and unbending principles,
the first of which is to be flexible at all times.
EVERETT DIRKSEN

A book about a family growing up with a monkey wouldn't be complete unless it included the thoughts and feelings of the other members in that family. Here then, in their own words, are what the men in my life have to say about life with Ziggy.

MICHAEL CAMPBELL, HUSBAND AND FATHER

I was the skeptic in the family. The kids were jumping up and down. "We're getting a monkey! We're getting a monkey!" And I'm thinking:

So who's going to clean up after this creature? What does it eat? What do we know about a monkey? Just what I need, the voice in my head went on, *something else to be responsible for.* But being married to Andrea, I have learned to expect the unexpected. Suffice it to say, if I had any arguments against the idea, I lost.

When Ziggy arrived, she was tiny, quiet, and non-threatening. She hung out on Andrea's wrist a lot. As time passed, though, she began to assert her personality on each of us. I guess she was setting up her hierarchy. To me, it seemed like she was trying to figure out just how much she could manipulate each of us into doing the things she wanted. I really didn't want to get attached to this creature and tried to deal with her as simply another responsibility. Yeah, right. Her soft brown eyes, the hugs, kisses, and most of all, intelligence sucks you in—there *is* a light in the attic! It absolutely amazes me, even today, how she can communicate her wants and needs no matter how dumb we try to act. Until you learn to treat a monkey like an intelligent creature, you haven't got a chance.

After Ziggy had been in the house awhile, I got into the routine of having her around; she was just the monkey that lived in a corner of my house. One day while I was at work, Andrea called to tell me she had to go out and take care of some business. She wanted to let me know Ziggy would be alone for awhile. She was leaving around three o'clock, and I would be home around five-thirty, six o'clock at the latest. It wasn't a very busy day at work, and I decided to go home early so Zig wouldn't be alone for quite so long.

I walked in the house around four-thirty. As usual, my head was still in the clouds. I looked to see if there was any mail and checked the refrigerator for a snack. At this point I realized Ziggy was awfully quiet. I called her name. Nothing. I moved closer toward the cage.

I couldn't really see anything. I hadn't turned on the lights when I came in, and the room was in shadows. As I approached the seven-foot-tall cage, I got a sick feeling in the pit of my stomach. Then I saw her. She was pinned upside down between the back wall of the cage and the iron grate flooring. Her feet were above the grate and her head and arms were hanging limp below. The way Ziggy's cage is designed, the iron grate stands eighteen inches from the bottom of the cage; Ziggy's poop falls through the grating onto a tray of cedar chips, which we remove and freshen on a regular basis. She must have been trying to lift the grate when she became trapped.

Ohmigod! I thought, *The keys, where are the keys? On the end table? No! In the box by the computer? Where's the box? Where's the damn box! There it is. Now, where are the keys? Why am I moving so slowly? Nothing is ever where it's supposed to be. There they are, four keys on the ring. Why in the hell do we have four keys on this ring? Which one is it?* My hands were shaking. *Come on, be the right one. No! Try again.* Click, the lock popped open. I ripped open the cage. I reached for the grate, slipped my fingers through the holes, and tried to lift it up. It wouldn't budge. *So much for this gentle stuff.* I reached down and yanked that grate so hard it popped up and smacked me in the head. Ziggy dropped into the cedar like a limp doll and did not move.

I was absolutely certain that Ziggy was dead. I reached down, lifted her up, and held her to my chest while I sat down feebly in the rocking chair. I just rocked back and forth, rubbing my hand up and down her back. She was not breathing—that much I could tell. I just didn't know what to do. What does someone do when the monkey he is responsible for dies in his care?

I remember thinking that Ziggy was warm. *If she was dead, why was she warm?* Then—*yeech!*—Ziggy started to heave up whatever her stomach held, all over my shoulder, and she continued to retch, throwing up all over me. What do I do now? Two things came to mind: First, take off this disgusting shirt; second, call the vet. Actually, I did both at the same time. There I was, holding Zig in one hand, the cordless phone between my shoulder and ear, removing my shirt with the other.

Most veterinarians do not have extensive experience working with monkeys. He probably didn't know much more of what to do than I did. He told me to get her down to his office right away. So off I went. I tore a clean shirt out of the upstairs closet in a quick swipe and made a mad dash out the door, into the car, and over to the vet, clutching Ziggy against my chest. I can just imagine what must have gone through Andrea's mind when she came home later and found the house in this condition. The side door to the house was wide open, cage door open with the grate ripped out, my shirt on the floor covered with monkey puke, and no monkey, no Michael.

I held Ziggy close to my chest as I drove. She clung to me and nuzzled my neck. It seemed to take forever to get to the vet. It felt as if I were driving through molasses.

When you go anywhere with Ziggy, you tend to attract a crowd. I realize that others mean well, but on this trip I was more concerned for *her*. Fortunately, they were expecting us at the vet's office, and we were ushered right in to see the doctor. They gave Ziggy a sedative. I'm not sure if they did that because she actually needed it or as a precaution because of their not being overly familiar with capuchin monkeys. They asked me to sit in the waiting room while they did their doctor bit.

This was the first clear moment I was able to think about what had happened since the silence in the house had turned into chaos.

I felt that Ziggy was probably going to be all right, although I couldn't be sure she hadn't damaged some internal organ, and I couldn't fathom a guess how long she had been trapped. People in the lobby kept talking to me, but it didn't seem to be getting through. My only clear thought was, *I'd better call Andrea.*

"Where are you? What happened? Is Ziggy all right?" She was agitated.

"Whoa, slow down. I think the Zigster's going to be fine, but I still don't know. Somehow she managed to lift the floor in the cage and, while reaching down, got pinned between the back wall and the grate. Maybe she was trying to escape. We're at the vet's now. I'll call you back when I know more," I explained.

I waited in a wooden, straight-backed chair with a rock-hard seat for approximately six-and-a-half years, or so it seemed. Actually, it was only forty-five minutes. I guess it seems longer when you are sitting there feeling guilty for not anticipating the danger in what had appeared to us to be a harmless cage setup. By the time they brought me in to get Ziggy, I'd come up with several ways to secure the grate so that this would never happen again.

The doctor had x-rayed Ziggy completely and didn't find any serious damage, but he said she was going to have one monstrous stomachache. He said to give her some 7-Up and just let her rest. She was still dopey from the sedative, so it was really easy to handle her on the way home. Which is exactly what I did—headed for home—right after I called Andrea to let her know we were on the way and that Ziggy was going to be okay.

Since that incident, we have made a few modifications to the cage. The grate is now wired down, and we had a new floor constructed out of aluminum, which weighs about 2½ pounds instead of ten.

But to this day, whenever we have to leave Zig alone for any length of time, I'm just not comfortable until we arrive home and I hear her chatter and make "hoo-hoo" noises at us for leaving her home alone.

If prior to this incident I had regarded Ziggy as a responsibility and had it in my mind to remain detached—that was over now. Maybe it has something to do with shared experience or something psychological like that; I just don't know. What I *do* know is that since then, she's more like another child than a familiar family pet.

I really enjoy watching the monkey deal with everyone in the house. Andrea would probably deny this, but it is absolutely amazing how similarly she and Ziggy react. One time Andrea was working on some project in the living room, Ziggy was busy in her cage with one of her toys, and I was on the computer, more than likely playing a game of some kind. Andrea had stacked a pile of boxes on a yellow chair positioned in front, and just slightly to the right, of Ziggy's cage. Suddenly, Andrea stood up, picked up the boxes, and swung around, sweeping the bundle within an inch or two of the cage at just about the height of Ziggy's head. Not surprisingly, the Zigster was freaked out. She jumped up on the bars yanking back and forth really hard (this is affectionately referred to as "cage rattling," an activity we try to discourage), and while doing this, used her jungle-oriented "What the hell do you think you're doing?" kind of scream (you have to hear the noise to believe it). Needless to say, this, in turn, freaked out Andrea, who proceeded to drop the boxes, jump back, grab a broom, bang on the side of the cage, and yell at Ziggy something like, "What the hell do you think you're doing scaring me that way!"

I thought to myself, *Yeah, I just bet that Ziggy knows exactly what you mean.*

I often wonder what Ziggy must think when Andrea or I are telling her something that she has not had any experience with. There's a water bottle contraption hanging on Zig's cage that she occasionally knocks down when she gets angry with us. The apparatus consists of a plastic bottle with two metal pieces designed to secure it to the outside of the cage bars. Once, when she knocked the bottle off, one of the metal hooks popped off and fell deep into the cage.

I point toward the metal piece. "Ziggy, get me the metal piece."

She looks up at me, probably thinking, *Why are you talking to me like I'm supposed to know what a metal thing is? I'll ignore him, maybe he'll go away.*

I say, "Ziggy, the metal thing. Over there!"

Ziggy looks back over her shoulder, *Hmm . . . He's not going away. I guess I'll run around the cage grabbing things and see what he does.* And as she is running around grabbing things, I see her touch the piece of metal wire. But being only human, by the time I can react and say, "Good girl, that's it!" she is holding Mr. Pearman, a plastic squeeze toy.

Noting my last reaction, she jumps up on the bars bringing Mr. Pearman with her, wanting to buss my lips and celebrate her success. "No! No! Not Mr. Pearman, the *metal piece.*" I point down to the bare wire lying in the cage, just inches out of my reach.

She turns away, and I think she must be saying, *"Jeez, there's just no pleasing this guy; what the heck is a metal piece anyway?"*

Yet, with all her running around in circles, she does manage to kick the desired item close enough to the bars for me to finally get it. Sliding it out of the cage, I say, "Good girl, what a good monkey."

She looks up at me as if to say, "Whew! I'm glad that's over. Now I can get back to grooming my best friend, Dirty-Stinky-Smelly Guy. (Want to guess why we call him that?)

For some reason, Ziggy regards me as the alpha male in the house. The plus side of that is that while she was going through her biting phase, I was never a target. But the upshot of the true situation—and one that everyone else seems to ignore with the possible exception of Andrea—is that *she is not as affectionate with me.* Ziggy will sit for hours with Andrea, cuddling and being stroked. If we have been away for any amount of time, it's Andrea she gets all excited to see and tries to entice to the cage for a welcome back hug. With me, she just wants to play-fight, but in a gentle sort of way. She rolls into a ball, mouthing my nose, lips, cheek, and ears. And she always wants to take me somewhere, like, *Daddy, let's go.* Plus, there are periods when she won't have anything to do with me for two or three days at a time. And she does like to groom me, too, but it is only on *her terms.*

The one question we are always asked is, "How are you going to deal with giving her up when Helping Hands calls?" All I can say to that is, if my sons, in their outward search for who they are, end up doing something half as worthwhile as Ziggy, I will be thrilled.

C O U R T N E Y   C O L L I N   C A M P B E L L , 2 2 ,   E L D E S T   S O N   A N D   B R O T H E R

(Author's note: Courtney calls his mother Andrea, and his father Michael.)

It doesn't seem so very long ago I was called downstairs to a family meeting. We didn't ever have family meetings *really;* I think it was parental code for: "Everyone has thirty seconds to prepare himself to completely restructure his life." I'm exaggerating, of course, but that is pretty much what it felt like most of the time. So I put down my book or video game and trudged downstairs.

I recall walking into the kitchen not quite knowing how big an event this was going to be, but I had a sneaking suspicion that it probably had something to do with us leaving dishes in the sink or water on the bathroom floor. When I arrived, the looks on their faces read differently, and I breathed a sigh of relief. My parents had the kind of expressions they got whenever they decided they were going to tell us something new and unusual. Andrea was looking around the table at everyone with a thin-lipped grin that broke into a wide smile every few seconds; and Michael glanced at us with a slightly bewildered look, as if he was ready to tell us something he didn't quite believe himself. *This is going to be good,* I thought. The last time they looked like this we opened our home to someone from another country—my foreign-exchange sister—who came to live with us for a year.

Andrea began, "We're going to be a foster family."

"Are we getting another exchange student?" Jordan asked.

"No," Michael said. "We're going to be a foster family for a monkey."

I sighed. It was turning out to be an interesting childhood.

One day several months later, my brother and I were left to watch a video and our parents departed, returning a few hours later with Ziggy. She was about eight inches long, and we all agreed she had a head no bigger than a golf ball.

At the time—I was about eleven—I was unaware of certain practical things: One, that baby animals are so cute it makes your teeth hurt, and two, that my family was in for some real-time adventure.

It is kind of like people who get romanced into buying a Labrador when it's a small, cuddly puppy, not anticipating just how big it'll get or what they'll need to do to train it.

That was how we felt the day we found out that Ziggy would bite. It was weird. We were sitting on the deck, doing things people do to animals that are too adorable for their own good, when out of nowhere, Ziggy bit Jordan. I had gotten nailed just like that already, and my mother got hurt, too, much later on. Most people can't really understand just what it means for a monkey to attack you. It's a lot like the *Alien* movies. They move almost faster than you can see. My perception at the time was that monkeys can be dangerous, lightning fast, and not give a care. At first, we were all confused and made excuses for her behavior. Ziggy didn't mean anything by it, of course. It was an instinctual reaction. Ziggy just needed to show us where we were in the hierarchy. And we needed to figure out where, why, and what precipitated an attack.

After the bite, order was restored. What was done, was done. And it was obvious to me that we were never going to be able to read the real reasons for its happening. It was then I started to pay attention to the differences between monkeys and people.

Ziggy, of course, doesn't realize that we're not nearly as quick as she is, or that in polite society it isn't nice to leave scars. To her, I think, it amounted to nothing more than simple childhood misbehavior with a purpose. In everything I've ever read about primatology or seen Ziggy do, it has not been difficult for me to see how the origins of primate behavior help them to survive. Ziggy, at a young age, was discovering for herself just where she stood in relation to everybody else. She certainly didn't intend anyone any real harm.

I've always been intrigued by her behavior. Her actions always had some innate purpose; I guess you could call it form following function. I could find no type of duty like that in my own life, at the tender age of whatever—near adolescence—at least none I was willing to admit. So I paid attention, and read. Mostly I just paid attention.

I noticed not only the *differences* between man and primate but also the *similarities.* In the big picture, there really aren't all that many differences; I'm sure of that. We lost a little hair, got a little bigger, learned to drive; hell, we've built cars, but we still have the same needs: warmth, food, love, and order. It's the *similarities* between us and the other primates that provide the most insights into our own lives. You can see *us* in the way they move. How they react is often nothing more than their acting out their hierarchical group structure.

On the other hand, sometimes when she does something really exceptional, I think it's the differences between us and other non-human primates that really shine a light on what humans have lost through our species' evolutionary gain.

Ziggy catches fruit flies, gnats, and little specks of what appears to be dust floating in the sunlight. Anything that moves overhead. What's strange is not that she does this (no, I take that back, it *is* strange), but that it is done *the same way* every time.

Ziggy will be minding her own business when, out of the corner of her eye, she'll catch something floating through the air. Then she sits up, furrows her brow, and with a look of concentration bordered on frustration, she attempts to pick the object right out of the air. The look on her face is always the same. Granted, there are times when she chooses not to chase after the object, but when she notices it, the same preying search crosses her face, even if she decides not to do anything about it. It's simply what is done when something has the audacity to be floating near enough to be noticed. For Ziggy there never seems to be any question of whether the offender *should* be plucked from the air, just the question of how it should be removed (as near as I can tell, I've never really had the opportunity to question her properly; that inability to form human speech is a bitch for her sometimes.)

After the object is plucked and eaten or has escaped, the preying look leaves her face, and with it, all thoughts about the deed. Oh, I'm certain from time to time it does occur to her, probably in her dreams. I have seen that hunter-to-quarry-look cross her sleeping face on a rare occasion. And on the rare occasion that a small bit of floating debris does escape her sharp brown eyes, no concern is needed. She simply picks up and moves on to where life takes her next.

Some of her habits are all "too human." When faced with a moral quandary, say, if the two primary caregivers are fighting or engaged in a quaint bit of verbal sparring, Ziggy naturally becomes perplexed. And in the same way men have dealt with moral quandaries or feelings of inadequacy since the time of Cain and Abel, she finds the nearest person who is weaker than her by nature and proceeds to antagonize.

I've seen this happen many times over the years. Someone in the house will snap at someone else, and moments later we hear the dog yip because she's just been scratched. A glance at the cage reveals Ziggy with her back arched and fur standing on end, glaring a warning to the dog. It is a mixed posture nonetheless, aggressive, yet combined with a look that begs for reassurance that all will be well again soon.

The dog was not the only one warned, by any stretch of the imagination. My best friend Kevin got nicked, and I have several scars myself. Certainly no long-term harm for any of us though. In her world, it is simply what is done to dominate. The fact that monkeys are equally quick with each other means it is no big thing to transgress in monkey society. But it has a tendency to make us humans more wary. It's interesting, too, in my mind, that the main difference between Ziggy's actions and human aggression would be the fact that Ziggy doesn't ever appear to question her reflexes and, most times, seems to have no residual guilt. She adapts quickly.

I still have trouble figuring out why people insist on doing the same bad things to other people when they know they should do better. Of course, human violence takes many shapes. We've come up with a thousand ways of taking out our social angst on others, from backhanded compliments to cutting people off on the road and slowing down in front of them. We've raised it to an art form, I'd say, none of which solves any of the problems that instigated the behavior in the first place.

And what Ziggy does best is to *forget* right after the altercation is over. She doesn't harbor any feelings of repressed bitterness or anger. She behaves almost as though it never happened. She wants to maintain order. She didn't strike out at the dog because she doesn't like her—it's not that calculated—she struck out because right then she felt confused and wanted something else to happen. Monkeys want everything to belong in its proper place. She may be reacting to a situation that, at its base level, threatens her survival. Because if the family unit falls apart, the species doesn't survive. But when the situation is over, things return to the way they were. Ziggy never stays angry, I think, because she never doubts that she will be loved. She has never known anything else from us. The concept of not being cared for has probably never occurred to her. We will be there for her because we always have, and as far as she's concerned, always will be. At least that's what I think.

Human beings have an amazing capacity to take the things that hurt us and make other people pay, long after the only thing that's left is a faded memory of the hurt, which was most likely unintentional in the first place. Ziggy is too honest for that. We humans carry the hurt and worry because we've learned to doubt that we're loved. We've learned to forget that we're cared for. Perhaps some of it stems from the fact that we no longer have to depend on each other to survive. I don't have to worry about me or my neighbor growing enough food to feed the family and live through the winter, and no one else I know does either. We just have to make enough money to buy the things we need, and that can be a solitary situation. Although this is a wonderful thing for most Americans—to no longer be worried about mere survival—with this new life format, we've lost a great deal of our community. We think we've found replacements for cooperatives, but I've never really gotten the feeling that television loves me back.

I've seen Ziggy wear a lot of faces: She gets upset, angry, and afraid. But later on it seems there are no bad memories; she's lucky. She doesn't get stressed out or have nervous breakdowns. I understand that some monkeys and apes in the wild have bouts of depression and fail to thrive in an environment that is being destroyed around them. They are confronted by a situation that they cannot understand, which threatens the only thing that is important to them, the colony. Ziggy *is* lucky. She knows neither real fear nor hunger, knows no human to be malicious, knows no real pain or loss.

The world to her is a bright place of happiness and warmth. It is good to be innocent.

My father says I have this talent. I try to remember that every day is a new day. I'd like to think I was able to do this as a child and somehow managed to remember it as I grew older. Michael was always surprised when, after a long family "discussion" (that's another word for *fight*), everything was okay with me. Even if it took days for everyone else to be at ease again, I was always able to turn it off, as if with a switch. I find, as I grow older, that becomes harder and harder to do. It isn't an easy thing; society isn't set up that way, what with bills, deadlines, and credit. It is difficult to remember how to let go. I think Ziggy can do it. She has no concern over whether bills are paid, no worries about getting enough food, and no wondering who cares for her. Just enjoyment for her life. Living not in the past or future, but in the eternally happy *now*.

In fact, today *I had a very good day*. I stayed up late with two of my good friends talking about whatever. As the sun threatened to rise, we all finally retired and later, in the lazy hours of late morning, we gradually awoke to each other's presence. After some coordination and a quick trip to the grocery store, we feasted on a Heinleinesque breakfast: sausage, bacon, eggs fried and scrambled, English muffins, apple cinnamon muffins, oranges, bananas, French toast, syrup, and jam. After doing our best to try to eat the massive quantity of food before us, we laid back like fat bears and noticed the sunbeams that streamed in through the undraped windows. As I watched the dust spin in the sunshine of a lazy Sunday afternoon, I thought to myself, *Ziggy has inside her what we spend our whole lives looking for—that which we simply forgot we had.* I imagined that every day in the whole world of her life must be like what I was experiencing right now. And that, I thought, isn't such a bad way to be.

JORDAN TAYLOR CAMPBELL, 19, YOUNGER SON AND BROTHER

What can I say about Ziggy? She's been a life-changing experience. I cannot imagine what our childhood would have been like without her. She is friendly and loving toward all her family members, especially now.

Like all normal families we've had our disputes, but we have always seen past them. And she is a confidant, my confidant, and has always listened to what was going on and being said around her. Most people believe she can't understand what I'm saying. That is completely and utterly false. She interacts and responds to everything I or anyone else says.

It's amazing, too, that she has helped me with some of my problems. She doesn't necessarily respond like a human would, but imagine having someone foreign in your house and neither of you know each other's language, but you are forced to live together for nine years. You will, no doubt, come to have an understanding of what certain words mean, and you can read the emotions of your friend, no matter what. That is what it is like with Ziggy. We may not know each other's tongue, but we damn sure know what each other is saying.

The years we've had Ziggy have gone by so fast, it's hard to believe we have had her almost a decade. Ziggy has been raised like me and has almost matured with me, seeing as how monkeys develop much faster than humans.

I've seen Ziggy do some things that are quite amazing. We had a problem containing her when she was about two or three years old. She would make a habit of watching us when we put her back in the cage and then do exactly what we did, in reverse, to get out. I don't mean simple tasks either. One time my father wound wire around the bars to hold the door closed, which he tied in several complicated knots that we humans would normally have a hard time undoing ourselves. Ziggy watched while he tied them together, then quickly, and I mean quickly and deftly, undid the wire, removed the snap-clamp from the door, and ran through the middle of the living room as we watched TV. The only other device we found that can truly keep her in the cage is a master-lock on the door. She knows how to undo that one, too, but we don't give her a key!

Ziggy has always been as cute as anything you can imagine. I used to use her to get all kinds of women. I called her my "chick magnet." I'd be talking to a female friend and the conversation would turn to Ziggy somehow. My friend would normally turn to Jell-O, fawning over the idea or the picture of Ziggy I showed her. Sometimes I'd invite girls over to see her. Most would eventually make the effort to come. Personally, I loved it—having all those beautiful women coming to my house. I've grown up somewhat, and now I usually pick the women I hang around with by noticing who *doesn't* make a fuss over Ziggy. It shows a sign of maturity when they don't start squealing and saying, "I want a monkey, too—can I see her?" It's almost a relief when an interesting prospect says something like, "Aww, she's cute," or "That's cool," and leaves it at that. It shows control.

It was always amazing to me how much Ziggy is like *us*. When people tell me they want a monkey now, I usually tell them that's like saying, "I want to have a kid." Because she is exactly like having a newborn, and then a baby, and then a child. You have to love and care for her, spend lots of time with her. You have to bathe, clothe, feed, and clean up after her; change her diapers; and teach her.

Despite the trouble, I could never have imagined my life without her. She *is* my sister. And I will always love her, forever.

When she leaves, a piece of me will leave also; one that will never be filled.

helping hands

I have trouble with toast. Toast is very difficult.
You have to watch it all the time or it burns up.

Julia Child

It was a wintry Boston day and I was bundled to the teeth. I made my way up the hill in boots that hadn't seen snow in more than twenty years and checked the address more than once. I don't know why I had expected the Helping Hands facility to be bigger; Judi Zazula, the executive director, had mentioned that they occupied a series of rooms within a rather nondescript building. As I got off the elevator and approached the door to the Helping Hands training center, I noticed there was a security keypad and, next to that, the doorbell. I stomped the snow from my boots and rang the bell.

Any anxiety I'd had about being in a strange city and any trepidation I'd had about meeting the people who held my monkey's future in their hands, vanished the minute the door opened. Judi greeted me with a monkey baby—TC, a fifteen-week-old female with an endearing and mischievous face—snuggled into her arms.

There are three sources of information for a foster parent in this "new generation" of Helping Hands. I call it a new generation because Helping Hands is celebrating its twentieth year in operation, and since the early years of my becoming a foster mother, the dedicated workers within this nonprofit organization have refined and honed the business to run like a well-oiled machine. They constantly push harder in order to provide the kind of services required for the monkeys as well as the foster parents and the handicapped recipients. The three sources of information for a foster parent are the monkey itself; Doreen Marchetti, the program's literal lifeline between family and facility; and the parents' own judgments and instincts.

Ziggy and I had been among the pioneers of the Helping Hands program. When we signed on to be a foster family ten years ago, we received few instructions and operated largely with common sense and gut instinct as our guides. Today, I would find out if my judgments and instincts had been correct over the long haul. This prospect was a little intimidating to say the least. Certain questions ran through my mind: Will Ziggy be as smart and as well-behaved as the others? Did I make any mistakes in my assumptions along the way? and, Would I be able to give my monkey over to someone else, knowing that I would never see her again? I felt like I was going to my child's school for her first progress report.

We entered Judi's office and I unpacked my gear for the day—camera, notepad, and a gift of a photo frame with a monkey mounted on it. TC scampered around the room, climbing, poking, acting like a hyper kid. For this reason, our conversation was punctuated by diaper changes, some quick kisses and hugs, a toke on a bottle of formula, and all the other little piddling chores required of a doting mother. This procedure itself, of Judi caring for the little ones, is new, too—Ziggy came to me at the ripe age of five weeks. Now, all the infants get a little bit of preliminary socialization at the facility (they go home in the evening with Judi) before they're placed into a foster mother's arms.

This new procedure makes sense for a couple of reasons. Although an infant like Ziggy becomes inseparably attached to its human mother, infants in Judi's care feel more confident among the community, have a tendency to venture out, and become acclimated to more than one special person. This method also allows the trainers and handlers an opportunity to begin the little one's report card. The new monkey's personality, proclivities, and temperament are noted by all. This, in turn, aids in the infant's transition to a new foster mother or father. The monkey's character is richer for its associations, and new parents are made aware of the monkey's individual nature—a component that cannot be overestimated when matching a monkey for placement.

Today, applicants go through many levels of assessment (which I had abrogated by being one of its earliest members). All prospective new parents must send in a video tape of their home layout, showing where the monkey will be housed, who all the members of the family are, and anything else they care to share on tape. Cages need to be approved by Helping Hands in advance, to ensure the safety of each cage and eliminate the possibility of any unnecessary cage-related behaviors, such as those Ziggy so cleverly demonstrated as a young monkey every chance she got. The building, design, expense—and later on, repair—of the cage is still the family's responsibility. It's like that theory: If you pay for a puppy and name it, it's more likely to be of value to the owner after the glow of newness has worn off. (Unfortunately, though, new families no longer have the option of naming their foster baby either.)

The future foster parents must be dedicated enough to make the trip to Helping Hands to claim their little charge in person. This introduction provides the organization with the opportunity to explain their goals and objectives, demonstrate the training, and reiterate their expectations and requirements. It also affords the chance for a family to "back out" if they feel that the commitment to time, money, and patience is too overwhelming.

Our progress out of the office and into the active "hub" of the facility was what I had been waiting for. Walking into new rooms and down the halls, one is very aware of the art. It is like a rogues' gallery; everywhere the walls are covered with pictures of monkeys. Monkeys galore. Some are wearing clothes, playing with toys, mooning the camera, in water, with their caregivers, talking, playing, working, loving—everywhere large photos, pictures, posters. Monkeys depicted in all phases of their life at Helping Hands.

Adept at presentations and the "dog-and-pony show" that is required of all nonprofits, Helping Hands has made signs and posted them at the entrance to the different rooms. For example, before entering the housing area, signs about acceptable human behavior and notes on methodology are posted. There is a sign that limits the number of guests allowed inside and makes suggestions about how to respect the occupants, for instance, by letting them reach out for you instead of you reaching out for them. After all, this is their private space, their *home*. Some of the monkeys are housed together; a few others prefer living alone. One reason for this is that their appetites may be such that they do not share food quite as willingly as others. (Anyone—human or otherwise—who has lived with multiple room-mates knows whereof I speak.)

The minute your face rounds the corner into their quarters, a chorus of cheers, squeaks, hellos, peals of joyous laughter, and effervescent life takes over and fills the air. There is really nothing quite like being greeted by a roomful of monkeys—monkeys who are well cared for, clean, bright-eyed, and keened up. It's wonderful. A radio plays softly overhead so the constant sound of human interaction is always with them. A television is mounted up above, too. It is a gift from one of the foster families who wanted to make sure that their little love would be able to watch his favorite programs.

The main room, where all the bills are paid and the computers hum, acts as the central command post. There is a life and energy here that is best experienced in person. It was not the usual bustle of activity, however, because many of the student helpers and volunteers were out for spring break. On the day of my visit, Laura, a volunteer student helper, was cleaning a cage; Jean was going over a tangle of forms; Sue, head trainer, was eating lunch; Nancy, the placement assistant, was preparing the monkeys' food. She was preparing to visit someone's home, packing equipment and advice. She will act as a touchstone for the program.

Later on, I parked my carcass in the main room and watched as different monkeys were tethered to the wall, in pairs, so that they could play on the indoor gym set, climb over the toys, or help Sue fold the laundry. Throughout the day, they take turns sitting on Sue's lap and just hang out—it's like a little "time-out" for Mandy, or Kerrie, or Sydney.

Every square inch of space is occupied with the accoutrements of life for monkeys. Closets are filled to overflowing with medicines, treats, utensils, housekeeping supplies, paper towels, soaps, mirrors and play boxes, artifacts of personalization, and clutter. A large hallway houses cubbies and shelves filled with the monkeys' favorite possessions. Like a day care facility in which the children have their name printed on storage boxes filled with their own special toys, hats, and mittens, these cubbies hold treasures that the individual monkeys have come to love. One monkey has a box filled with soft toys, and Judi pulled out a rather strange looking stuffed love-mate called a "Buffalump"; this was some monkey's idea of a favorite companion. If they have a beloved dish, toy, or item of clothing, it is clearly labeled with the owner's name and rotated among their other toys during each cage cleaning.

The guiding principle here is that *each monkey is an individual,* and although they may have similar species characteristics, their personalities are what drive their behavior. All the workers know every monkey's name and idiosyncrasies. Helping Hands knows they must provide for each monkey's singular and distinctive character because doing so will not only aid the monkeys in their training, but it also demonstrates that these dedicated human handlers have an abiding love for the animals. That love is clearly evident to me in every phase of the operation.

WHAT IT'S ALL ABOUT

If I had to pick one word to sum up Helping Hands training, I would have to say it's *amazing. Mirabile visu,* wonderful to behold. I'm told the most-often heard comment among visiting foster parents is, "I can't believe my monkey will ever do that."

The monkeys are introduced to training through a series of three rooms. The first room is no bigger than a walk-in closet. It is narrow with low-level lighting. It is soundproofed and moderately free of design except for a monkey-stenciled border ringing the ceiling. The sound-proofing assures that the environment will be relatively distraction-free, and the low-level lighting ensures that the laser—a beam of light, like a flashlight but more concentrated—will be noticed.

In here, the monkeys learn to touch a red-painted block that is adhered to a white wooden board. Later on, that red block will simulate the red-dotted item that the monkey will either press or push on to manipulate and facilitate the operation of a VCR or similar item. On the other hand, a white dot pasted on an object is something they are encouraged to avoid. A white-dotted item could be potentially life-threatening, such as a medicine cabinet or something as innocuous as the telephone, a trash barrel, or even a plant. There is very little pressure on the monkeys to perform at this stage. If the monkey even just so slightly touches the red block, they are rewarded with hugs, verbal praise, and a treat. This room also contains toys, stacking blocks, and things to turn, place, and play with.

The second room is approximately the size of a small bathroom, about eight-by-ten feet. There are pieces of equipment, some working, some nonfunctional. In here the monkeys continue to learn tasks of manipulation, again with the laser stick, but this time the objects are real: a microwave, a board with light switches mounted onto it, a row of cassettes and the machine they go into, food holders for human beverages and snacks, and more. Much of the equipment has been donated and some of it does not work, but it is adequate enough to use for teaching—like a simulated cockpit for a pilot, it won't fly, but the principles are the same and it's good enough for instruction.

It was here that I learned that Judi and her husband, Doug, a physi-
cist, have actually engineered some of the items the quadriplegics use.
Judi has an extensive background in occupational therapy and rehabilitation engineering, while Doug has an impressive knowledge of
science and how all things interrelate. Their unique collaboration has
resulted in a number of innovations that help handicapped individuals
do more for themselves with and without monkey assistance. Judi and
her husband have spent countless long evenings designing equipment.

Because of Judi's welcomed entry into the quadriplegic individual's home and lifestyle, people would talk to her about their needs
and the shortcomings of their environment. She would take their
ideas home and try to create what they required. One such device,
remarkable in its ingenuity, is the sandwich box. It is basically a plastic sandwich saver box with a lid. It is attached to a slim rod and
when that rod is placed into a stand, the box is laid open, exposing
the sandwich, which is held intact by nylon screws.

Judi and Doug have not only not taken time from their own lives
and unselfishly given it to others, but their devotion to Helping
Hands and the monkeys has evolved into a true lifestyle commitment. Whatever the monkeys and the people who share their lives
need, they have devoted advocates in Judi and Doug. When these
two individuals take stock of their lives, I believe they will have no
regrets, because these are the choices they have willingly made, and as
different as their lives are, with monkey activities at the forefront,
their love for the animals is strength-renewing, a mission. Most people do not live long enough to create such a purpose for their lives.

The third training room is the largest. This one is not soundproofed; by this point the monkey should have learned the play-tasks
well enough to not suffer the kind of distraction that would keep her

from completing the assignment. This room looks an awful lot like a scene set, as in a play, and, indeed, it is the setting of someone's home—a quadriplegic's. In addition to a hospital bed and cranky old wheelchair, it contains the comforts of life that make up a home: a picture frame with a photograph of a paralyzed person and his monkey, a telephone (with white dots on it signifying nonmanipulation), a flower arrangement, a lamp, and other artifacts of daily life. The only thing that sets it apart from most other disabled persons' homes is the monkey's cage.

On the day of my visit, we watched Sue, the trainer, work with a monkey named Cocomo. Sue climbed into the wheelchair. The wheelchairs are manipulated with the aid of a chin control; this enables the owner to power the vehicle around and into different spaces. (This particular model was a bit broken-down, but Judi said it's important that the monkeys learn to "ride" on machines that aren't the Cadillac of the trade, so to speak, in preparation for whatever model of wheelchair they'll find in their new home.) To begin, Sue issues the slightest command, distinct, but neither loud nor commanding. Cocomo moves from her perch on the back of the chair onto the counter. Sue gives a one-word request for a drink. Cocomo climbs down to the floor, goes to the mini-refrigerator, retrieves a water bottle from the shelf, and brings it to Sue. They drive to the desk area together. Cocomo positions the drink on the desk, opens it, and inserts a straw. Sue uses a small squeeze bulb to dispense a fruit drink into a shallow depression of the wheelchair-mounted treat dispenser. Cocomo takes her drink; she's been a good girl. Simultaneously, Sue gives the monkey lots of verbal praise.

I watched as additional commands were drilled, for tasks such as fetching a sandwich, putting a cassette into a machine and turning it on, displaying and opening the pages of a notebook, retrieving a mouth stick that has fallen to the floor, repositioning limbs that are hanging or pushed too far forward, scratching an itch on Sue's face, and so on. Although the monkeys are not tethered—completely free in their homes—they can hook their own small leashes onto the chair for a ride to another area or room. I think my favorite part, and also the most surprising, was watching Cocomo return to her cage, close the door behind her, and defecate before coming out again.

There were some minor sidebars. Cocomo took the opportunity to cross the room, climb over my arms like a bridge, and onto Judi's shoulders for a hello and some loving. Monkey diversions are tolerated (once she even pretended there was something scary under the bed), but the diversions are minor and brief, and the trainer waits patiently for them to complete their routine—while giving them a gentle reminder of their tasks. It's a very patient and compassionate procedure. There are no shock belts, no loud or extreme noises. The commands are soft, usually one or two words with easily distinguishable sounds between them. The simple fact that these monkeys are trained without using any of the fear-based techniques used by some animal trainers in other venues gives further credence to the notion that the monkeys *love their tasks.* This is a brilliant, agile species that wants to please; they perform their tasks in exchange for a sip or two of a sweet fruit drink, and prompt, reassuring words of praise.

I came home from Helping Hands with several ideas. I learned how to alter Ziggy's diet so that she can be the "healthiest" monkey possible. I brought home medicine to help heal a cut on her tail. I also gleaned tips on how to train her to "fetch," to let her know yet again the joy of learning a new task. I also learned not to let her play with the buttons on the remote control, the telephone, or the calculator.

She may have to "unlearn" any confusing habits later on. I came back with renewed confidence, knowing that my monkey is not only on the right track but she will one day become a star pupil herself, like Doreen's "Einstein" Emily, who can do it all at eight years old!

My trip to Helping Hands also gave me some much-needed insight. Now I know that when Ziggy goes to school, she will be in good hands. As painful as it is for foster parents to give their little monkey sons or daughters up, there is comfort in knowing that the monkeys will be loved by everyone at headquarters. Every monk that comes and goes leaves a lasting imprint on the trainers' and helpers' lives—and pierces their hearts when they leave them, too.

placement profiles

Accustom thyself to attend carefully to what is said by another,
and as much as it is possible be in the speaker's mind.

MARCUS AURELIUS

This quote from Marcus Aurelius, one of the great Roman emperors, may be an important piece of advice for someone with a career in public service, but I doubt very seriously if his adage would apply to the interviews I conducted with two wonderful individuals on the Helping Hands program, Sue and Tom. There is no way I could expect to climb into the head of someone who has suffered the trauma of becoming a quadriplegic and thrived in spite of it.

In order to give readers a well-developed picture of why we foster families work so hard to raise the best little monkeys possible,

I felt it was important to write about some of the recipients of Helping Hands monkeys. I do not know where Ziggy will end up, whose life she will go on to enrich, who will be the beneficiary of her love and assistance. The ache that my family and I will feel in giving her up will be tempered by the knowledge that she will immeasurably improve the life of someone less fortunate than ourselves. If there is one point that should be made here, it is: *this is the end result.*

I'd like to point out that in addition to the physical tasks the monkeys perform, there are other, less obvious, benefits to the handicapped participants in this program. First, there is a psychological lift in having a companion, one that neither makes judgments nor tires of its tasks. I believe I can safely say that the people who receive the monkeys don't want to feel needy. Asking for help for every little thing must be a bother. Having a monkey companion grants the recipients autonomy—it allows them some time *to be alone.* With a monkey aide, they do not have to depend on a caretaker almost continually.

There's another sideline benefit: The monkey creates a kind of "celebrity" status for the recipient and a distraction from the wheelchair. People who are reticent about talking to a wheelchair-bound person for fear of not knowing what to say or saying the wrong thing will more likely strike up a conversation if a monkey is involved. It provides a starting point for discussion and tends to put people at ease. This can be an enormous benefit, particularly if the handicapped person feels isolated. There's nothing like having a monkey to get a little more attention!

SUE AND HENRIETTA

Sue is fifty years old. She was twenty-two when she was injured. She was traveling to California with a few friends. They had stopped for lunch, gotten back on the road, and Sue went to sleep. The rented van they were driving had not been maintained properly by the rental company and they'd gotten as far as Pennsylvania when the steering mechanism snapped and the van veered off the road and rolled over.

The other passengers suffered cuts and bruises. Sue got the worst of it. When she regained consciousness in the hospital, dazed and afraid, Sue found she was agreeing to have a physician insert a trachea tube to help her breathe. After a time, she learned she was paralyzed.

Sue logged six years in a long-term-care facility until she was able to live independently, in her own apartment, but not without the support of various aides who came in to help her bathe, get dressed, exercise her limbs, transfer her from the bed to the wheel-chair, help her to eat, and perform her other daily activities. With characteristic optimism and unbroken spirit, Sue says she coped with what was happening to her by taking things "day by day."

One of the early participants in the program, Sue was introduced to Helping Hands through one of the hospitals in her area. Helping Hands was still in its research phase when they put out feelers to occupational therapists, looking for a recipient for a monkey. The feelers led them to Sue, a thin, dark-haired, quiet girl who had gone through so much.

I asked Sue what she thought about the first time she saw Henrietta, her monkey helper. She said, "I thought she was small." And the most surprising thing? "To meet an animal that had hands."

Sue's typical day involves the time-consuming activities surrounding her survival. An attendant arrives in the morning to help prepare her for the day. Sue breathes with the aid of a respirator, and everything must be cleaned and checked to ensure her safety. She reads and also spends time on the computer and manages to work for the library. When I asked if she had too much time, she responded by explaining, "There's never enough time. Because if you have to rely on someone to help you do things, you have to factor in the extra time to get it done." Sue told me that if there's one outstanding thing she has learned from her injury, most of all it's taught her patience. "I had never known patience," she says.

Sue's monkey, Henrietta, has an interesting background. Henrietta is from Oregon and had lived with another woman for ten years as a family pet, and as a consequence, her teeth had been removed. After a time, the woman donated her monkey to the wildlife society with the stipulation that she not be used for research. Henrietta could not go to a regular zoo because the other animals would endanger her, so she was sent to a children's zoo. This situation did not suit her sensibilities, however, as the children visiting the zoo startled her. Henrietta's caretakers looked for another alternative and called Helping Hands. (Helping Hands will try to take in other monkeys if at all possible, and has become a safe haven for appropriate monkeys from research or pet situations that are in need of a new home.) Henrietta found love and direction under the guardianship of Helping Hands.

Today "Henry" does the typical day's tasks for Sue, picking up things that have fallen to the floor, bringing her companion juice, water, and tea; and most importantly for Sue, retrieving the mouth stick, which enables Sue to manipulate various other objects. Henrietta also, Sue told me, ". . . lies around, looking adorable."

Because Henrietta was fourteen years old when she came on board, that would make her thirty-two-years-old now, a senior monkey. I asked Sue what this meant, and she told me this: "Henry does not like toys—she is an adult. She was taught to drink from a glass and put it down when finished; she will wipe a table with a sponge;

and mail—she loves to open mail—she has her own basket for mail. If someone brings her a new stuffed animal, she will first check it out to see if it will eat her. And next, she will see if *it* can be eaten and, if it's not food, forget it."

Sue enjoys the occasional interview and has represented Helping Hands on the board of directors and been the subject of many magazine articles over the years. Occasionally she will give classroom talks for teachers of graduate programs at NYU, answering questions about her life with her monkey, but she will not bring Henrietta along. Instead, Sue will bring a video of Henrietta at home. Henrietta does not enjoy going out, and crowds are stressful for her. Sue told me that the monkey will go out onto the terrace for a look, and that the folks who come in will groom and play with her; that is enough for her.

I asked Sue how Henrietta showed her love. Sue said that she makes chirping noises, will rest on her arm, lie in her lap, and emit a throaty purr similar to a cat—the deepest of contentments—but that most of all, she shows her love by being *reliable*. Henry helps to "eliminate the elements of accidental happenstance," as Sue puts it; a character trait that makes for Sue a reliable, stable home.

Tom and Mango

Tom is thirty-eight years old. He possesses a dry sense of humor, and his friendly voice has an engaging, distinctive drawl. He was an active sixteen-year-old when his accident occurred. Tom was a passenger in a friend's car and was not wearing a seat belt. It was a cold Saturday and they had been coyote hunting. Sometime after lunch, they were heading back into town when they approached an intersection with a slight downgrade in the road. Their vehicle began sliding, about five miles per hour, skating on a sheet of ice. A semi-truck, an eighteen-wheeler, broadsided the car. The driver was pushed from the car, leaving Tom pitched toward the driver's door, when he got hung up on the post. The driver suffered a broken collarbone. Tom, who was in and out of consciousness, was hurt very badly.

After the accident, Tom went through a stage where he wondered *Why?* He claims he suffered a little depression but it was fleeting, and he doesn't know why it didn't progress either, despite the poor facilities. The hospital services were dismal at best and the quality of care was not there. He was low on blood, developed a terrible bedsore, and lost his breathing. It frightened his parents because they were told he would live out his life in a hospital. His mother wouldn't accept that assessment and kept checking out different facilities and hospitals until he got transferred to Minnesota, where he received better care and had access to rehabilitation therapy. The mood was even better in Minnesota; they were always moving other people into where Tom could talk to them.

Then, finally, the day arrived when he was able to get around on his own in an electric wheelchair. But from the time he went into the first hospital in January, until he got into the final hospital, it was already deep into November.

Tom and his family discovered Helping Hands while listening to a television news show. They hurried to get a paper and pencil—but to no avail—no address was given. Still, the seed was planted. Over the years, they had an increasingly hard time finding good attendants, so hard in fact, that Tom's mother was feeling pretty burned out. It was then they remembered Helping Hands. They just knew that a monkey helper could give his mother some of the relief she needed, and a monkey could help provide Tom with what it was *he so desperately wanted*—companionship. Tom couldn't believe his luck when he got Mango.

Mango is a little boy, sixteen years old, ". . . a mature monkey," Tom says, and he's had him for six years. I asked him to describe Mango's character and Tom said this: "Mango's a shy guy and he likes things quiet." (Like Henrietta, he, too, is a homebody.) "He enjoys staying home and taking care of me." I asked Tom how he knew this and he said, "I can just tell." Mango is a snuggler, and Tom has a perch on the back of his wheelchair so Mango can cuddle up against his neck to watch TV. Mango likes Connie Chung, but he hates David Letterman and especially dislikes it when Howard Stern is a guest.

Mango performs tasks such as picking up things that have dropped to the floor, replacing the mouth stick, helping Tom with the phone and computer, putting in VCR tapes, retrieving books, repositioning his hand onto his chair, and getting Tom drinks.

And what about objects of his own? Mango's preferences lead to certain toys that move and click. He is partial to transformers, and the wrestling guys with arms that go around and around and make small noises.

I learned that Tom's day is active too. It takes a long time to get him ready and going; his day begins at eight o'clock. There are a range of exercises to be done (for retaining motion and preventing atrophy and stiffness). After his personal care and a change of clothes, he eats. On alternate days, he gets a shower. I asked him what the injury had meant to his character and disposition, and he said he's more patient, more mellow. If he had to choose, Tom told me that the biggest difference and the best thing that Mango brought into his life is the independence and the confidence that comes with having him.

Tom's family is supportive and he lives with his parents. His two brothers are off with lives of their own. And Tom does a lot of work. He is an active member of the Jaycees, the Junior Chamber of Commerce, and he works on a variety of community projects. Using his computer, in the past he helped to run the baseball program in his community, which boasted five hundred kids. His duties included hiring the umpires, making arrangements for the coaches, scheduling games, and finding sponsors for thirty-five teams. He also took part in the awards ceremonies. Tom is currently chairperson for the annual Fourth of July celebration in his area. In this capacity, he arranges for the pyrotechnics, orders the fireworks, raises money for the festivities, recruits volunteers, and delegates the work. In addition, with the aid of his computer he also e-mails friends in the service who are stationed in Korea and Germany. And whenever he's involved with his computer, there's Mango, to help him make it happen.

"If I need to move papers, I don't have to wait for my Mom to finish with supper," Tom says, adding, "the vet is here locally, so Mango never has to leave me, and when I go for checkups at the hospital, he comes to visit, and all the nurses and attendants know him and can't wait to see him." Tom said that people are often afraid and intimidated by his wheelchair and that Mango's presence helps to break the ice, but, he also added, they still like to "keep a low profile."

Tom hates the cold, dreary days of winter; he says that Mango "has a way of just making the winter days fly by." With a voice full of emotion, he says, "Mango makes me happy, I *am* happy. Mango loves me and I love him. He is my son. When I got him, I sent out birth announcements."

Gotta love me: Ziggy seems to know just how cute she is.

The boys, Courtney *(top)* and Jordan *(bottom)* with their "Zigster."

(top) Animal magnetism: Ziggy demonstrates her attraction to Marc Brown, a visitor to our home. Thankfully, Marc was a good sport! *(bottom)* My husband, Michael, came up with Ziggy's name. If he named her, I figured we were well on the way to acceptance of the idea.

Ziggy has shown me that each and every day holds new wonders to behold.

Ziggy's first birthday party. Since she was born on our anniversary, May 14, it was a dual celebration. The cake read "Happy Birthday, Ziggy" on one side and "Happy Anniversary" on the other.

We made a ceremony out of bath time. Grooming is very important for primates and Ziggy is no exception.

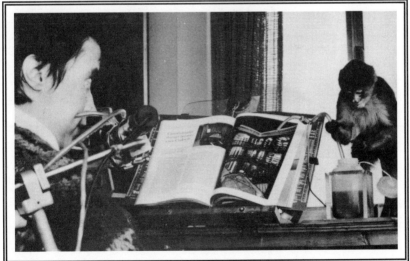

Devoted companions: Sue and her monkey helper, Henrietta.

epilogue

May the best of your past, be the worst of your future.

UNKNOWN

Having Ziggy has not only been an enriching experience—a once-in-a-lifetime dream—but she has also added to my life in a much richer way. By the very fact that Helping Hands has allowed me this honor, I'm more cognizant of her and her species. I always want to learn more about primates. I read all things primate, collect stories, and amass tchotchkes that look like primates. I would be remiss then, if I didn't address the concerns of primates in our larger planet.

In our quest for progress and a better way of life, humans can inadvertently be a destructive and manipulating force against our planet's natural environments. As the world's population increases and more nations make movements toward progress and, thus, destruction, we must all think about being more careful about what we touch, move, or alter. We are closing in on all the virgin territory left in the world. It is becoming harder to find unspoiled lands. And the future of many types of primates is being threatened as their natural habitats are dwindling away. We need to think ahead. If we can't stop the destruction, we need to plan on creating sanctuaries for displaced animals and help them to live their lives with the least amount of disruption possible. We may one day be caretakers for them all.

In the print version of the *Multimedia Guide to Non-Human Primates,* author Frances D. Burton writes, "While still widespread in South America, *Cebus apella* is threatened by habitat destruction and conversion of forest to commercial use. Hunting for food and capture for the pet trade has been made illegal in some countries of its range. While the species is protected in national parks and reserves, these are not adequately monitored. Tufted capuchins are used as bait to capture big cats and are killed as vermin where they raid crops. In the late 1960s, over 7,000 of this species were exported to the U.S. and nearly 1,000 to the U.K. for biomedical research."

The fertile jungle belt in South America, Central America, and Africa is being eaten up. Commercial logging companies slash and burn their way through it, and individuals clear fields to farm or establish homesteads. This kind of destruction often leaves the scorched earth unable to sustain any life, and the cycle continues: more chopping, more movement, more burning. Unfortunate, but true. We may, one day, be responsible for all of those species who are driven away or cloistered into smaller and smaller areas that are unable to house and nourish them. And I cannot do anything about that situation except to read, discuss it with others, and perhaps write about the problem with an eye to a solution—with a lifeline to hope.

My knowledge of primates has evolved over a significant time and been shaped by my burgeoning desire to build a legacy for these fabulous creatures. I have been bolstered by the total support of my family and aided by the people within Helping Hands; I can't tell you how important this has been. The experiences in this book are mine and my family's, and they do not reflect on the way the Helping Hands program is structured today, or probably the way it will be tomorrow.

I still *do not* know it all, and I am continually challenged by what is left to learn. Just this year I had to sew a bag for Ziggy. She got a cut on her tail, and the sore was located in such a convenient spot that she would pick the scab off over and over, to her amusement and my dismay. The only way to solve this particular problem was to make a bag from a flannel king-size pillow case. Doreen at Helping Hands helped me to figure it out. I cut down the length somewhat, made a casing and threaded a drawstring through it at the waist, and finally, created some tabs to hang the whole thing off her belt. So, in essence, she is *inside* a skirt that is closed at the bottom. I had imagined that Ziggy would never be able to navigate like this—ho, ho, was I wrong—she moves without a second thought! Doreen had told me about another monkey who wore a similar garment to distract her from a bandage. She perfected her own navigation by walking "on her hands." They are so clever.

This year was Ziggy's first exposure to crayons. The routine here is simple; we open the box, take out the crayon, peel the paper, open the box, take out the crayon, peel the paper, open the box . . .

Amazingly, she colors without breaking the crayons, better than some elementary kids I know who can't resist. As for style? She doesn't care *what* she draws, so long as they are sherbet colors.

And there is always room for a new adventure. One day when Ziggy was in the car with me, as part of the day's chores, I filled the car with gas and ran it through the automatic car wash. She was not a happy passenger. When the soft fringed sponges came down to snake across the windshield, she freaked. It had never occurred to me how foreign and frightening that would be for her (and it didn't get any better through the rest of the process). In the future, scratch automatic car wash from her "things to do" list.

Now matter how mundane we think our lives have gotten, Ziggy has shown me that each and every day holds new wonders to behold if we will just open our eyes and hearts. I hope this book helps you to realize some of your own wonders and gives you better insight into what we can do to give value to other primates' lives.

about the author

Andrea Campbell has studied primatology for over a decade—including her hands-on experience with Ziggy. In another field of interest, she has a degree in criminal justice and is the author of *Rights of the Accused* and *Forensic Science: Evidence, Clues & Investigation*. Her other books include *Your Corner of the Universe: A Guide to Self-Therapy Through Journal Writing* and *Great Games for Great Parties*. She writes a weekly human interest column for *La Villa News* and *La Villa Express*. She resides in Hot Springs, Arkansas.

Helping Hands is a national nonprofit organization dedicated to improving the quality of life for quadriplegic individuals by training capuchin monkeys to assist them with daily activities. They provide these special monkeys, the knowledge about them, and lifetime support, at no charge to disabled individuals.

If you would like to make a donation, their phone number is:
(617) 787-4419

You can visit their Web site on the Internet at:
www.helpinghandsmonkeys.org